THE END OF
MAJOR COMBAT OPERATIONS

by

NICK McDONELL

McSWEENEY'S BOOKS
SAN FRANCISCO

www.mcsweeneys.net

Copyright © 2010 Nick McDonell

Cover and interior photos by Nick McDonell.
Front cover: U.S. Infantry and Iraqi civilians, west Mosul.
Back cover: Five soldiers of A Company in the 3-8 Cavalry, Forward Operating Base Marez;
Iraqi National Police and detainee, west Mosul.

All rights reserved, including right of reproduction
in whole or part in any form.

McSweeney's and colophon are registered trademarks
of McSweeney's, a privately held company with
wildly fluctuating resources.

ISBN-13: 978-1-934781-96-8

Printed in Canada.

Don't brush the flies from the wound
My wounds are the mouth of Job
My pains are patience waiting
And blood seeking revenge.
O Lord of the poor workers
We were not defeated
The giant peacocks alone were defeated
Quicker than the flicker of a flame.

—Abdul Wahab Al-Bayati,
from "Lament for the June Sun," 1969

Gustavo Nogueira, "Gu," twenty-two years old. I asked him about *it*, the same thing everyone asked me about when I got home. Some people came right out and said "Did you see anyone die?" Others wanted me to tell them the worst thing I saw. Gu didn't care about any of that. He was an extremely light-skinned Brazilian and in the short time I knew him spoke frequently about how people could never figure him out. I couldn't either, at first, but not because he looked like a white boy, called the black guys in his platoon *nigga*, had a south Boston accent, and sang in Portuguese under his breath. I couldn't figure him out because he was a decent guy who, if he didn't take pleasure in killing, didn't seem to mind it that much.

Gu was a sergeant in the United States Army serving with the 1st Cavalry Division in Mosul. When he started his first tour a few years ago, getting shot at every day in Baqubah, his mother didn't even have her papers. She was working as a housekeeper in Boston, an illegal alien. Gu himself didn't want to stay in America much longer. He wasn't in the Army for citizenship, like a lot of his Fijian or Samoan counterparts. He was an American citizen already, but he was also a citizen of Brazil. He had a plan to move to the beach back in Rio, drink rum, and fuck Brazilian chicks, two at a time, from every direction, balls deep, all day long, forever.

In the meantime, though, he thought the Army had made him a better man. Maybe it had. He was no dummy, Gu; he wasn't wasting any time, even if it looked like he was just talking shit and smoking. Of all the soldiers with the 1-12 there in south Mosul, he was the one who was picking up the language. He'd be out at night, knocking on doors and scanning retinas, and he'd say *What's up* in Arabic and the man stepping out of the house might smile and the kids at his legs would go wide-eyed. Gu would stick out a combat-gloved hand for a high five, crouching down in his fifty pounds of full battle rattle, saying *Salaam alaikum, little player.* I don't know whether it made them less afraid of him or more. On "census" missions like that he was really just going around getting people out of their beds at night and demanding information. It wasn't like anyone could say no.

But then it wasn't like Gu could say no at that point either. Fuck all the girl soldiers in the back of a Bradley he wanted—*He actually did it, the motherfucker*, another sergeant told me—he had to follow orders. In fact, as a sergeant, he had to *give* orders sometimes. Though he never expressed a doubt about anything we talked about, sometimes you could see in his smirk that he almost couldn't believe he'd been given authority over other men. But he carried that authority fiercely, and five years and two tours in, he knew about orders. As for why he did it in the first place—signed up for the business of killing people and destroying things—it had to do with drugs and not wanting to work a shitty job and being bored and, actually, seeing an Army recruiting video. He told me he knew it was cheesy, but when he was eighteen and saw those light-infantry guys with their faces blackened, running into the middle of some shit-storm in the jungle, he thought, Damn, that's me. I can do that shit.

And he did, in Baqubah. Door to door, orange mangrove to orange mangrove. It is much easier to sympathize with Gu and the friends he lost than with the people they were fighting, like the al Qaeda chief Abu Musab al-Zarqawi, who was killed just north of Baqubah by a pair of F-16s after several years of bragging about beheadings. Baqubah was a stop on the Silk Road in Iraq's Diyala province, but in 2007, for one hundred and nineteen of Gu's comrades, sixteen in his own company, it was the last place they ever saw.

It is also much easier to sympathize with Gu and his company than with the government that sent him into battle, the particularly incompetent Bush administration—though the Bush administration was really just another iteration of a republic that had been at war, more or less, since its creation. Still, it was the Bush administration that bragged about the war, called it *bringing democracy* when in fact it was much more complicated and sinister than that. Gu called what he did killing, not democracy, and he didn't brag about it except to say he was good at it.

Which he was. A brave, well-trained soldier in the most powerful army in history.

II

Transit Points. The Starbucks in Queen Alia International Airport in Amman, next to final pre-boarding security. Sprawled out on a bench across from posters of pastry is an extremely sunburned bald Caucasian, dressed in the brown and tan of security contractors and romantic tourists. Walking by, you can hear him snore, napping at the outermost edge of his influence. On the other side of the flight, waiting on the ramp from the plane, he isn't safe in the same way. His influence concentrates down into the tool in his hands, the gun that was waiting for him as he drove to the airport, pushing past the streetlamps, orbs of light floating in the dust, through an all-day twilight as alien to his Southern-boy roots as the first muezzin's call, like copper through the air, that woke him up that morning in a hotel room that looked like hotel rooms all over the world.

III

From *The U.S. Army/Marine Corps Counterinsurgency Field Manual*, (Field Manual No. 3-24/Marine Corps Warfighting Publication No. 3-33.5), Chapter 1:

Contemporary Imperatives of Counterinsurgency

I-137. Recent COIN experiences have identified an important set of additional imperatives to keep in mind for success.

MANAGE INFORMATION AND EXPECTATIONS

USE THE APPROPRIATE LEVEL OF FORCE

LEARN AND ADAPT

EMPOWER THE LOWEST LEVELS

SUPPORT THE HOST NATION

...

Paradoxes of Counterinsurgency Operations

I-148. These paradoxes should not be reduced to a checklist; rather, they should be used with considerable thought.

SOMETIMES, THE MORE YOU PROTECT YOUR FORCE, THE LESS SECURE YOU MAY BE

SOMETIMES, THE MORE FORCE IS USED, THE LESS EFFECTIVE IT IS

THE MORE SUCCESSFUL THE COUNTERINSURGENCY IS, THE LESS FORCE CAN BE

USED AND THE MORE RISK MUST BE ACCEPTED

SOMETIMES DOING NOTHING IS THE BEST REACTION

SOME OF THE BEST WEAPONS FOR COUNTERINSURGENTS DO NOT SHOOT

THE HOST NATION DOING SOMETHING TOLERABLY IS NORMALLY BETTER THAN US DOING IT WELL

IF A TACTIC WORKS THIS WEEK, IT MIGHT NOT WORK NEXT WEEK; IF IT WORKS IN THIS PROVINCE, IT MIGHT NOT WORK IN THE NEXT

TACTICAL SUCCESS GUARANTEES NOTHING

MANY IMPORTANT DECISIONS ARE NOT MADE BY GENERALS

And so on. Maybe these imperatives, straight off the page, could be useful to observers of counterinsurgency, too. Encourage us to "use the appropriate level of force" in criticism, never mistake a frightened man for a malicious one. To "support the host nation," even if we don't speak Arabic. I would like "to learn and adapt"—to learn, perhaps, that isolating the ephemera of a complex and bloody war, a field manual, for example, is an easy way to criticize an institution, and an old trick. But I still look at the guidelines, the laws, the manuals. The U.S.'s top general, David Petraeus, Commander of CENTCOM, said this of the one excerpted above: "Surely a manual that's on the bedside table of the president, vice president, twenty-one of twenty-five members of the Senate Armed Services Committee, and many others deserves a place at your bedside, too."

There has never been a bedside manual for observers of counterinsurgency. Michael Herr's *Dispatches* is probably the closest we've got. "In Saigon," begins one chapter, "I always went to sleep stoned so I almost always lost my dreams…"

So one last look at the COIN manual, maybe off the bedside

table, before stoned sleep, at the opening paragraph of the intro-
duction by Sarah Sewall, Director of the Carr Center Program on
National Security and Human Rights at Harvard's Kennedy School
of Government:

> Those who fail to see the manual as radical probably don't understand it,
> or at least don't understand what it is up against.

IV

The people you meet on the plane. A frightened woman who must sell her family's house in Monsour. The DOD contractors. The nephew of Adnan Pachachi, a prominent Iraqi parliamentarian. We got to talking, in quiet voices, slowly, about what we were doing in Baghdad. He worked for OPEC in Vienna and would be in and out in ten days, he said, had only been in Iraq three times in the last thirty years. Being there was like touching fire, he said. If the U.S. leaves it will be slaughter, and the notion that Iraq is stable now is propaganda. And his uncle should have been the prime minister but he was tired now and anyway they didn't want him.

"Who?"

"Anyone."

He had some business to do and then he would be back in Vienna as fast as he could be. I was going for a rotation as a correspondent for a news magazine. Talking to him made me wonder if the only things all of us on the plane had in common were money and the blood in our veins. As we began our descent, the frightened women, Iman, asked another woman, in the row ahead of us, if the woman might help her find a good taxi, or a safe bus, to get into the city. The woman in the row ahead said no, she could not help, and turned back around.

"I guess they cannot trust anyone anymore," Iman told me, and looked out the window, through the dust, at the vast rows of tan military tents.

V

One story I worked on in Baghdad began over the neon crowds of Times Square, in the New York headquarters of Reuters. The office was carpeted, quiet, smaller than you expected it to be. City light poured in through the windows but the faces of the staff seemed to be illuminated in equal measure by the screens they stared into.

I was there to meet a friend of a friend who had been in Iraq. He hadn't stayed very long, but was generous with his contacts and enthusiastic about the trip I was about to take. He urged me to look up the young man who had been his fixer in Baghdad, Hakim. The friend of a friend told me that Hakim knew everybody and everything.

Hakim had moved to Queens. He responded quickly to the email I sent him, and suggested that we meet at a coffee shop in Long Island City, near his apartment. It was a weekday morning, warm for February, and I arrived early and took a seat by the windows. A couple of Hispanic guys, construction workers, it looked like, were picking up coffee to go. Otherwise the place was empty, so it wasn't hard to pick out Hakim when he walked in. At large in the city, of course, he could have been anybody. He could have been a Lebanese guy from Bay Ridge, or a Palestinian, like the guy who runs the bodega on my corner in Williamsburg. There are around seventy thousand Arabs living in New York City according to the last census, in 2000. Two hundred and two of the Arabs there now are Iraqi refugees admitted to the United States in 2006. One thousand six hundred and eight more, including Hakim, were admitted in 2007.

He wore tight, iron-gray jeans, a sweater, and several silver rings, one of which, he told me later, had been blessed by Ayatollah Sistani.

Hakim was a large man and dark. Though he was clean-shaven, I had the impression that I could actually see his beard growing. He looked older than his twenty-four years. When I met him, he was studying conflict resolution at Columbia University. He had received a Fulbright grant, and we talked at first about universities and the Fulbright program, which awarded money to scholars to facilitate "mutual understanding" between America and the rest of the world. It was named for J. William Fulbright, the Arkansas senator who'd founded it in the mid-forties, a few years before he signed his name to the Southern Manifesto opposing the Supreme Court's decision in *Brown v. Board of Education*. Hakim was a student of American culture, and curious about everything American. He had a job as Middle East producer for *Good Morning America*. He thought of himself, in part, as a New Yorker.

When we finished our coffee we walked toward the condominium tower where Hakim lived, and he told me some of his story in the wind blowing off the East River. His father had been a deputy foreign minister under Saddam, and an ambassador posted abroad. Thus, Hakim had spent significant parts of his childhood in Lisbon, Dar es Salaam, and Dodoma before returning to Baghdad as an adolescent. He spoke Portuguese, Swahili, and English, as well as his native Arabic, and he had distinguished himself quickly as a good student in one of Baghdad's private Ba'ath schools. He remembered meeting Saddam for the first time around the end of high school— though his father had told him he'd met him once before, when he was a little boy. It was around the time of this second meeting that the Ministry of Information identified Hakim as a promising recruit. He began working for the Ministry during his final year of high school, when he was seventeen. When the regime allowed foreign journalists into the country, Hakim was sometimes assigned to show them around.

This was his job in the spring of 2003, when the Americans invaded. As soon as the Ministry of Information disintegrated, Hakim began to hire himself out as a fixer to the journalists he had previously been chaperoning. They paid much better. Off-hours he studied at Baghdad University, but his real education, the one that would make his career, happened between Kalashnikov rounds as he looked for stories and trouble with a constantly rotating cast of Western journalists.

Hakim's Queens apartment was high in the tower, looking across a whitecapped East River to the Manhattan skyline. It was bare of decoration except for a few photographs and a pair of mortars, arranged shrine-like beneath the large windows over the river. Hakim said that they were the only souvenirs he had brought back with him, that doing so had earned him twelve hours of detainment at a New York airport. The punchline was that he was an immigration official's worst nightmare: an Iraqi national with stamps in his passport from Afghanistan, Pakistan, Syria, and Jordan, carrying a pair of unexploded mortars. But it was worth it to get them into the country, he said. And of course there was no reason to worry. He supposed if you dropped them out the window they might explode, but otherwise no way.

One of the photographs in the apartment was a framed headshot of a little girl in a headscarf. It rested flat on a dresser, as though Hakim had been looking at it recently and then laid it down. I asked him about it, and he said she was his adopted daughter. She was living in Turkey now. He trailed off, and I didn't say anything else about it.

We looked at other photos on his laptop and talked about how difficult it was to get into the U.S. even when you weren't carrying unexploded mortar rounds. "I even had letters from Diane Sawyer and Charles Gibson," said Hakim. He listed other prominent journalists he'd worked with as he clicked through pictures he'd taken since the beginning of the war. It was a gruesome slideshow. If Hakim was not a great photographer, he was a direct one, and not squeamish. The picture I remember most was of one man holding another's decapitated head with a look of terrible grief on his face, as though he wanted to hold the head and stroke it and comfort it, but was too repulsed by it and so was holding it at arm's length. Hakim didn't narrate.

We discussed possible stories. I had mentioned that I thought it would be interesting to practice with a Baghdad basketball team, since I was a long-suffering Knicks fan and leaving New York while they still had a chance of making the playoffs. As it turned out, Hakim had been captain of the Baghdad University basketball team for a year. He knew the right people, and he would introduce me to them over email.

I was grateful for this, and I asked Hakim if there was anything I could do for him. There was. He had some things he wanted to send to Amman, but shipping them would be too expensive; he asked if I would carry a bag for him. I said yes, absolutely.

Two days later, Hakim and a cousin of his arrived at my apartment out of a wet evening, rolling a large suitcase full of gifts— shoes and clothes, Hakim said—for their family. The idea was that I would leave it with the concierge at the Four Seasons in Amman, where *Time* put up its transient correspondents, and then an uncle of Hakim's would pick it up. Does that uncle live in Jordan? I asked. No, Hakim told me, he would be driving in from Iraq. There were relatives in Jordan, but this bag wasn't for them.

The cousin with Hakim was Iraqi, too, recently arrived from Jordan. His father lived there and ran a successful dentistry practice.

If you have any need for a dentist, the cousin told me, contact my father, everyone knows him, his office is just off the Fifth Circle.

"His father was Saddam's dentist," Hakim told me as I walked them out. The cousin said that sometimes, when his father worked on Saddam, the bodyguards would unholster their pistols. He had adopted his father's profession and moved to New York to open his own practice. I wished him luck and left them at a Thai place nearby. We all agreed to play basketball sometime.

Back at my apartment I looked at the suitcase. Then I opened and emptied it, setting each of the small plastic bags within on the floor. As Hakim had said, it contained children's clothing, shoes, a necklace for his mother. I packed the bag back up.

It occurred to me, as I emailed Hakim's basketball friends in Baghdad that night, that I never would have gone through the bag if I was delivering it to someone in the United States. I thought about this again that first week in Baghdad, about the way people trusted each other or not. His friends hadn't emailed me back, but grasping for connections and ideas about the city I emailed them again, called, left messages. It was going to be a story about basketball, but really it was going to be a story about the occupation.

VI

For a novice in Baghdad, it was hard to tell what was a taxi and what wasn't a taxi. In the end, a translator for an American magazine told me, if you needed a ride badly enough, every car in the city was a taxi. This is an interesting idea to think about in Manhattan, maybe in front of the Council on Foreign Relations on Park Avenue, where the meetings would likely start late if the cabs weren't yellow, and every time you flagged a car down you had to hope the driver was a decent man.

VII

I stayed in *Time* magazine's house, in a good neighborhood called Karada. It was a house of unfamiliar sounds. The several clocks on the wall and their dissimilar rhythms. The hiss and bubble of the water pipe we smoked as we played chess in the evening. The tapping of the keyboard in the front room that one of the guys was always playing computer solitaire on. The whir of the generators, constant and maddening if you got caught up in it. And every time the security guys walked through the door there would be a dozen seconds of metallic clicking as they cleared their pistols. They did this without breaking stride, usually—clearing the chamber, dropping the magazine, and depositing the nine-millimeter in the filing-cabinet drawer as they walked through the front room to the kitchen for a tea. The house was full of guns. There was a sort of wardrobe that the correspondent I was rotating in for pointed out to me on the first day. He explained that this was where all the guns were, and if it ever got really "serious" then this would be where to get a gun. In his years in the house he had only ever done so once, when small-arms fire had enveloped the neighborhood. It was right outside. He said that he and the security guys and the photographer had all taken a gun and sat in the living room, smoking and looking at each other until the fighting died down, and then they had put the guns back. Of course, the security guys didn't keep their pistols in the wardrobe; they kept them in their filing cabinet in the front room. Another sound: the metal scrape of that cabinet, opening.

VIII

On Friday, February 27, 2009, President Obama addressed the Marines at Camp Lejeune, in Jacksonville, North Carolina. "Today I've come to speak to you about how the war in Iraq will end," he began.

> I can announce that our review is complete and that the United States will pursue a new strategy to end the war in Iraq through a transition to full Iraqi responsibility. This strategy is grounded in a clear and achievable goal shared by the Iraqi people and the American people: an Iraq that is sovereign, stable, and self-reliant... Under the Status-of-Forces agreement with the Iraqi government, I intend to remove all U.S. troops from Iraq by the end of 2011.

A few weeks later, in March, the following statement was posted on the Sunni extremist website *al-Shoura*, which translates awkwardly as "the Consultative Council":

> First stance: After the American people admitted that their army was defeated in Iraq, and their military and economic losses were enormous, they voted in an unexpected way for a black man and they accepted that the slave of the House to be the master of the House (White House), this happened because this slave promised them that he will bring back to them their missing sons and properties, and will realize their hopes and dreams. And this is the new master's turn to avow the failure and defeat even if implicitly, he tickles his ancient masters/new slaves of the word "withdrawal" and honorable return of the greatest army in the history according to his saying.

It is not surprising that there were competing interpretations of
Obama's announcement. The history of the U.S. presence in Iraq is a
history of contested interpretation.

In 1986, for example, the United States Senate approved the
International Genocide Convention. Interpreted strictly, the convention would have called for intervention by its signatories to stop
Saddam Hussein's al-Anfal campaign against the Kurds. But it took
the Senate nearly three more years to agree on the details that would
incorporate the Convention into U.S. law, and by then Hussein's
army had already destroyed four thousand Kurdish villages. So U.S.
ratification didn't matter much. But when does the letter of the law
matter, if you don't believe your government is bound by it? What
difference, really, does a modification to a convention make, a new
interpretation, a little editing, the narrow space between "failure and
defeat" and "withdrawal and honorable return"?

"So to the Iraqi people," said Obama, later in his speech,

> let me be clear about America's intentions. The United States pursues no
> claim on your territory or your resources. We respect your sovereignty
> and the tremendous sacrifices you have made for your country. We seek a
> full transition to Iraqi responsibility for the security of your country. And
> going forward, we can build a lasting relationship founded upon mutual
> interests and mutual respect as Iraq takes its rightful place in the commu-
> nity of nations.

The Iraqis I met in Baghdad were wary. There was again room
for interpretation. Or at least, more room than there was to interpret
the end of the speech. Obama wasn't just talking to the Marines of
Camp Lejeune.

"God Bless the United States of America," he concluded.
"Semper Fi."

IX

Most of the interpreters—*terps*—working in Baghdad were hired by contractors, not directly by the DOD, and this is how it had been for Nabeel. He was hired by Titan Corp., the San Diego–based company famous for pleading guilty, under the Foreign Corrupt Practices Act, to bribing the president of Benin. Most of its business was not in West Africa, however; it was in providing translation services to the U.S. military. This is what Nabeel did, for four years. He interpreted for kids from Colorado and Vermont as they sped through Sadr City, taking fire. He interpreted on days when whole outfields' worth of American servicemen were killed all around him, sometimes in only a few explosive seconds.

In the beginning, right after the invasion, it was a great job. He didn't even hide his face behind a scarf, the way some terps did to conceal their identities. Even as the situation deteriorated, he thought he would be fine, barring truly bad luck, because he lived far from the base he worked out of, on the other side of Baghdad, and lied about what he did. He took alternate routes to work. But then he came home one evening and his wife had found a note slipped in through a window threatening to kill them all. So Nabeel took his Kalashnikov and his pistol and his wife and children right then and he walked out into the street. He hailed a taxi at gunpoint and drove to a relative's house. He hoped the problem would end, like he hoped the war would end. He went back to work. He believed in what the Americans were doing, he had loyalties to the men he worked with. The money was better than what he could get doing any other job.

On the day two of his children were kidnapped, his American colleagues did not arrive to help with the search as quickly as he would have liked, but they searched and they promised him blood. By some miracle, for reasons still unclear to Nabeel, his children were released by the militia soon after and discovered walking the broken street less than a mile from where they had been abducted.

After that, Nabeel moved his family onto the forward operating base. He hadn't wanted to do that—living on the base alienated his wife and children from their community. But he didn't feel like he had a choice. They moved into the basement of an outbuilding.

In this, the Americans were generous. They certainly did not have to let Nabeel move his family onto the base. But Nabeel had been with them since the beginning, and was a serious asset. He even helped them vet new terps, which was difficult work; as everyone said, it was hard to know whom to trust. The horror story for the Americans happened on Forward Operating Base Marez in Mosul, where a terp walked into the dining facility wearing a suicide vest.

Besides the vetting, Nabeel had distinguished himself by saving the life of an American, pulling him from the wreckage of an exploded humvee in which the man was bleeding to death. And later, on the day Nabeel's own humvee got hit, an American did the same thing for him. Nabeel's leg had been crushed in the metal of the truck; he knew, he said, that he was going to lose it. They had to cut him out. He'd also known, right then, that the captain who was sitting in front of him was going to die, because he saw the man's back open up as they took him from the truck and onto the stretcher.

When he woke up, he was in a hospital in Erbil, in Northern Iraq, and it wasn't like in the movies, where he could just turn his head and see his comrades in the next bed, or call to the nurses and ask about them. The nurses didn't know. The other guys in the truck had been flown straight to Düsseldorf for treatment there, and it wasn't as though anyone would be making long-distance phone calls from the hospital in Erbil.

It was around that same time that Titan Corp., having been bought by L-3 Communications (2008 revenue: 13.9 billion USD), was replaced by Global Linguistic Solutions as the primary provider of interpreters for Operation Iraqi Freedom. As Nabeel was recovering, Titan was removing its assets from Iraq. By the time he was taken back to Baghdad, one leg gone, the insurance money the company owed him was coming in from abroad, and was thus delayed. He got about seven hundred dollars every two months. But he wasn't worried about the money—he was sure he could make money—he was worried about walking. The doctors had told him that with the right treatment, he could probably move his remaining leg, and that, with a prosthetic, he'd eventually be able to walk again. But the treatment was unavailable in Iraq. He built a ramp to allow his wheelchair in and out of his basement apartment on the American base, but he didn't intend to stay. He intended to go to Europe or America and walk.

It was slow going. Titan Corp. was gone, of course, and did not return his calls. And the battalion he had been serving with when he'd been hit had gone home, too. He sent emails to all his friends and commanders, asking how he could get to the U.S. Many of them wrote that he was welcome in their homes when he arrived, but that they couldn't help him with a visa themselves. They were just soldiers. Had he tried talking with immigration services?

He had. He had shown them the same documents he was about to show me. Nabeel leaned forward in his wheelchair and stubbed out his cigarette. A friend had wheeled him in, and now he motioned to the other man without looking at him, in the unthinking way of a surgeon reaching for a scalpel. The friend carefully handed him a plastic bag. Nabeel unwrapped it and took out a folder. Inside the folder was more plastic, and inside that plastic, documents. Commendations from colonels, copied emails from lieutenants back in America, duplicates of medical reports. Nabeel had a story for each one, and each one was in praise of Nabeel.

He lit another cigarette. *So.* He believed there was still a chance he would walk, but he understood from the doctors that the chances diminished with every passing day. His other great concern was the welfare of his wife. *Pressure* was the word he used. She is under great pressure, because she must help him wheel up and down the ramp to the basement apartment on the foreign base. She must care for the children. She must find a way to make some money as well, because they do not always have enough.

When he finished Nabeel exhaled smoke and said, "When will my story be in *Time* magazine?" He was disappointed when he found out that it wouldn't. He looked as though he had thought that that was what the meeting was about. I hoped that the fixers hadn't told him this. Misunderstandings were common.

Nabeel shook his head and chuckled and stubbed the cigarette. "I will tell you something funny," he said, leaning to one side of his wheelchair. The American soldiers in his unit had started feeding some dogs in Sadr City just before he got hit. They had sort of adopted the dogs. Technically, soldiers weren't supposed to have pets on the base, but for whatever reason the sergeant and lieutenant and captain and whoever was around had let one pair of puppies slide.

"And the soldiers who kept the dogs," said Nabeel, "they had to fill out some paperwork, but they even found a way to bring the dogs home with them, to the United States."

X

The Madrassa al-Mustansiriya is the oldest school in Baghdad. It has taken the breeze off the Tigris through its narrow windows and wide arches since it opened in 1234. At that time three hundred or so students studied religion, philosophy, and medicine in its bright courtyard and shaded enclaves. When I visited, it was almost empty. The last students to set foot there were children from an elementary school, who had walked the cells on a field trip before the war began, in 2003.

Someone at a government ministry had continued to put money into the building, though, and so a dozen middle-aged ladies swept the courtyard and stone halls every morning before they settled into the visitor's center to sip tea until they went home. Their leader was Sohel, ready with a yellowed brochure. She said sadly that she and the eleven other women who were paid to care for the building were bored and did nothing, but this was not true. The Madrassa al-Mustansiriya was the cleanest place I saw in Baghdad.

It was also one of the most intact. The Mongols nearly razed the school in 1258, but the Americans had spared it in 2003. Sohel credited this miracle to the school's single, diplomatic security guard. He lived there with his wife and children, but Sohel told me I could not meet him. Even when pressed, she would not tell me why. How did he save the school, then? I asked.

According to Sohel, as the Americans were rolling into the city, a fedayeen ran into the school's courtyard and told the guard: "I want to set up a sniper position here, and martyr myself if I need to." The guard talked the young man out of it, like this: "If you fire with a rifle, they will respond with bombs and destroy this place." Which we might have, like the Mongols might have in the year Oxford University turned ninety-one.

"It is still dangerous here," Sohel said, leading me across the courtyard. Her son and husband had seen a suicide bomber explode in Monsour the day before, she said, and the traffic was awful. "No, the place is not safe as long as there are checkpoints every ten meters." She threw her hands in the air.

A single spent Kalashnikov shell lay on the ground of the courtyard, and I knelt in the sunshine to pick it up.

"Where did it come from?" I asked Sohel.

"It fell from the sky," she said. "Do you want to go to the roof?"

Passing through the halls and up the stone staircase I noticed in one of the cells a mattress, a pair of sandals, half a bottle of water. I didn't ask Sohel about it. On the rooftop we admired the view of the city, the maze of alleys, the river, the buildings on Haifa street that had been the walls of the valley of some of the fiercest street battles of the war.

As we walked the perimeter of the roof I asked Sohel to tell me more about the guard and his family who had protected the building.

"The guard is an honest person, and nationalistic, and he loves doing the job that he is doing," was what she told me as I knelt again, this time to pick up an empty bottle of ouzo on the roof of a seven-hundred-and-seventy-five-year-old Muslim school.

"That is it," said Sohel.

XI

If an American soldier dies in combat, the United States military provides his next of kin with one hundred thousand dollars, tax-free. During World War II, it was six months' pay, based on rank. But it may be that thinking about how much a man's life is worth to his family is about as useful as thinking about the differences, for a soldier, between a "popular war" and an "unpopular war." I did not know my grandfather, a lieutenant in what was then called the Naval Air Corps, but I suspect that as he was going down in his F6F Hellcat in 1944, he would not have thought these comparisons useful at all.

One hundred thousand dollars is a lot of money, though. Twice as much, for example, as the fifty grand it costs (according to one terp I knew) to buy yourself the rank of major in the Iraqi Army. Seemed expensive to me, but I only ever interviewed one Iraqi Army major while I was there, and I didn't ask him about it. His name was Ibrahim Mohammed Abdullah, and he was a stout middle-aged man with a bristling black mustache. I met him at a ceremony south of Mosul marking the transfer of authority over the local Sons of Iraq from the U.S. to the Iraqi government. The Sons were irregulars, former militias, who had been coopted by the U.S. in the middle of the war. The fear was that, since the Iraqi government would pay less, the Sons would switch sides (again, in some cases) and join the insurgents. The other fear was that the money just wouldn't make it down the corrupt Iraqi chain to the men at the bottom. Major Abdullah would not talk about those fears, though, or any questions of payment or money. We spent the morning listening to speeches about how well everything was going, and what good friends, what brothers the Iraqis and the Americans were. What Major Abdullah did tell me was this:

"We are very happy that our good friends are leaving."

Another soldier there, a twenty-year-old named Ahmed, told me that whatever the problems might be, it had been an easy decision for him to join the Sons of Iraq. He joined for the money, which was good: two hundred and fifty dollars a month, or, that March, about eight dollars and six cents per day, per soldier.

XII

Six years after the war began, everyone agreed that the Green Zone, home of the U.S. Embassy and the Iraqi government, was still nothing like the rest of the country. Journalists still described it as "heavily fortified" and "removed" and "another planet" and "Disneyland." American soldiers who lived and worked inside asked you what it was like "out there."

In this way, the Green Zone became emblematic of everything that was cowardly, arrogant, and dangerous about the Bush administration. Those who tried to break down the barriers were paralyzed by the bureaucracy, or worse. When the UN envoy Sergio Vieira de Mello insisted on leaving the doors open, as it were, at the UN's compound outside the Green Zone, a car bomb promptly took his life. After that the UN sent most of its people to Jordan, and bunkered the rest inside the Green Zone. They stayed in the private school that the children of Saddam's cronies had attended. Political officers and administrative assistants did laps through the narrow corridors, which ran a square around a sparse garden in the center of the building, and the lame sexual tension of international bureaucrats was magnified by collective immobility.

Maybe if the Green Zone had been split up from the beginning, divided into smaller pieces and scattered across the city, the alienated Sunnis wouldn't have been as eager to kill the politicians. Maybe. What was certain, though, was that six years into the war the experts agreed that the insulation was working against the Iraqi leadership. Hawks in DC could pass around *Imperial Life in the Emerald City* and other dissections of suited diplomats in army boots, but over there the central government was still a removed, troubled, and heavily fortified Disneyland.

At the same time, it was difficult to look in the face of anyone who had been there long enough to have lost friends and tell them that too much *force protection* was the problem. Maybe that was why it wasn't surprising when, in the spring of 2009, McClatchy reported this, under the headline IRAQ REDUX?:

> The White House has asked Congress for—and seems likely to receive—$736 million to build a new U.S. embassy in Islamabad, along with permanent housing for U.S. government civilians and new office space in the Pakistani capital... The scale of the projects rivals the giant U.S. Embassy in Baghdad, which was completed last year after construction delays at a cost of $740 million.

XIII

The occupation had its own language. A few weeks before I flew to Baghdad, I attended a dinner with a former official in the Coalition Provisional Authority who was also a writer, and planning to embed in Afghanistan the following month.

"With the first ID," he told me.

"What's the first ID?" I asked.

He raised his eyebrows. "You have to know what the first ID is," he said, as if he was disappointed to learn I was so uninformed, and sorry for me, too. "First Infantry Division."

There was a lot of language like that. You could hear a whole conversation of acronyms and proper names and not have any idea what had been said. It wasn't a vocabulary that anyone taught you beforehand.

One evening I stopped in the doorway of a former agricultural college because I saw the young Brazilian sergeant, Gu, standing and smoking with a couple of buddies. The building had been taken over by the 1-12, and they were talking about how they might or might not ship their gear home. Gu had a plan to slip his *burner* into some kind of trunk or otherwise smuggle it back.

"What's a burner?" I asked.

"I thought you were from New York," said Gu. He grinned widely and hefted his M4 up. "You don't know what a fuckin' burner is? A gun, man."

Hajji was a stranger appropriation. In Arabic, the term is an honorific indicating piety, someone who has made the *Hajj*, or pilgrimage to Mecca, to worship at the *Kaaba*. The Kaaba is the ancient cube that sits on Islam's holiest site in the center of the Grand Mosque. It is toward this cube that Muslims turn to pray. The Qu'ran states that Abraham built it. *Kaaba* was a word that I never heard in Iraq, though—and what Hajji really meant was enemy, like Charlie meant Vietcong, or Sammie meant Somali, or Jerry meant German. Diminutives, to suggest your enemy was like a lost child who needed to be disciplined, or maybe just blown the fuck away. Loaded words.

But most of the slang was simple. Vehicles were *victors*. Helmets were *kevlar*. A full set of gear was *full battle rattle*. Planes were *birds*. Helicopters were *helos*. Mine-Resistant Ambush-Protected *victors* were *MRAPs*. The Dining Facility was the *DFAC*. A Tactical Operations Center was a *TOC*, a Containerized Housing Unit a *CHU*. The acronym for "improvised explosive device" was *IED*, but more often you heard about *VBIEDs*, or Vehicle-Born Improvised Explosive Devices, pronounced vee-bids, or *SVBIEDs*: Suicide Vehicle-Born Improvised Explosive Devices. Suicide vest was shortened to *S-vest*. Interpreters were *terps*, and Lieutenant Colonels were *LTCs*. When they were promoted to colonel it was a big step, and you said they got their *full bird* in reference to the eagle insignia that denotes that rank. Cointerinsurgency became *COIN*, which had a poetic resonance with the "coins" that could be awarded by the battalion commanders. Coins were sort of the step below medals, the kind of thing that the LTCs and the colonel had to sign off on. One of the captains I knew made his own out of thick cardboard as a joke that no one thought was funny, because you usually got them for *taking contact*. The Iraqi Army was the *IA*, the Iraqi Police was the *IP*, the Ministry of Interior soldiers were *MOI*. A quick-reaction force was a *QRF*. Operational Security, which was emphasized on flash-art printouts posted next to computer terminals, was *OPSEC*.

And everyone who went there had to learn the language of the war, and did, and thought that it was new, generational. But the language wasn't new, even if the words were. It was old, maybe the oldest language there was.

XIV

There was an American correspondent compiling an oral history of
the war who was about to get married. He did his interviews inside
the fortified bureau. It was still considered dangerous to do long
interviews in many of the neighborhoods. It was possible, of course,
with the proper security and reconnaissance. Actually, it was possible
for a Western journalist to go anywhere, if he or she wanted. The air
would not solidify, stop you walking out the door. You could take
your chances.

But this particular correspondent did not have anything to
prove. He had snuck through alleys with insurgents, jumped out of
helicopters with Marines, "finished work that day with my clothes
covered in blood," as I remember him saying once. But he was in
love now, looking forward to his wedding. So for the oral history
project, he was prudent. He had a team of fixers and translators he
trusted deeply. The way it worked was that he would ask them to
find someone who had been at the Battle of Najaf in 2004, for example, or someone who had been shot by Americans in April 2006,
and then to bring this person to the house. On a day when the fixers
couldn't arrange anything, he might go and cover the fake reopening
of the National Museum, or a press conference in the Green Zone, or
a car bomb. But very few of the stories got into his magazine at that
point. They all ended up on the website. The correspondents saw
this as a problem and talked about it—*journalism is different now*—at
length. The recurring ideas: no one cared about the war anymore,
bloggers were ascendant, the economy was fucked up, the resources

were moving to Afghanistan, and violence had decreased. All true. The small-arms fire in Baghdad had lessened, and there were only three to four unreported explosions a day, according to a police commander in the neighborhood in which this correspondent was living. All the same, his fixers and security guards were pleased that he was willing to have them bring the interview subjects to him for the stories, rather than vice versa. That way no one might identify the subjects or their escorts with a Westerner and try to kill them.

One day the fixers brought an old man in, and the first thing he said was: "I left Baghdad a bride, a beauty. I came back to a widow." This was also the last thing he said, before he left. It was a good line, and anyway, sometimes the stories were very short, even shorter than that, just a word or two. Like *bride, widow*.

XV

Hakim's basketball friends sent me an email the day I finalized my embed with the 1st Cavalry Division in Mosul. They were Tariq, who wrote the email, and Ra'ad, who was cc'ed. They invited me to play in their Thursday basketball game, provided I came without any cameras.

It was unfortunate timing. The embed approval had required a stack of paperwork and dozens of emails between various Public Affairs Officers, and I was scheduled to fly north that Thursday. I decided that it would be much easier to reschedule with Tariq than with the various Public Affairs Officers, so I wrote back that I couldn't make Thursday, could I please come for a game when I returned from Mosul? I didn't hear anything from Tariq or Ra'ad for some time after that, but their first response had taken several weeks, and so I thought nothing of the silence.

XVI

A reporter friend and I were on the roof of the bureau, trying to get the portable satellite working before I brought it to Mosul. He had been coming to Iraq for nearly three years and urged me to have faith in what I saw and thought. It was a kind thing to say. There were so many different stories that it was easy to think that if you didn't see the very worst of everything, you were somehow unqualified to talk about the war.

Some stories carried the kind of weight that could make a private stare straight down into his mashed potatoes rather than look at the sergeant who was telling it. Or maybe not telling it, just wearing the First Marine patch that meant he had fought in the battle for Fallujah. And at the same time that sergeant, like all the guys who *had* been there a long time, would often believe that everything was incomprehensible, random or mystical. In spite of the trillion-dollar hypervigilance, the Kevlar contractors, the cell-phone jamming systems, most twenty-three-year-old American noncoms in Iraq would tell you that every time you rolled out, there was a chance you were gonna get hit, and if it was your time, it was your time. It was up to God. Which was funny, like it is in every war, because that's exactly what the other side was saying, too. Except we never said we were fighting on God's behalf. We said we were fighting for Freedom.

Anyway, maybe it was up to God. I talked with a former member of the infamous Mahdi Army who told me that he had witnessed miracles at the Battle of Najaf, that the bullets of the Americans had passed through the Mahdis but done them no harm.

On the roof, we couldn't get the satellite working. We had a cigarette instead. "Nobody has a monopoly on knowledge," my friend told me. "You have to know that." After the smoke we went downstairs and he loaned me a better flak jacket than the one the magazine had given me.

"So you don't look like an asshole," he explained.

XVII

Layovers. The difficulty moving around theater was one of the distinguishing differences for reporters, it seemed, between this war and Vietnam, in whose history we looked for legends like we were trying to read a map. It seemed that, back then, any journalist who wasn't a total asshole could just jump on a helicopter and fly out over the jungle in any direction. In my limited experience in Iraq, getting onto a helicopter could take two days. As a journalist you were almost always the last in line for what were called Space-A, or space-available flights. All the contractors, from the kitchen guys to the mercs with their customized SIGs, were ahead of you. There was always a crowd in the shack, as every helicopter-dispatch building was called. Sometimes the shack resembled a commercial airport. More than once I saw large groups of Southeast Asians and East Africans in secondhand body armor wheeling suitcases across the tarmac as though they were emigrating to somewhere other than Baghdad, or the next DFAC they'd been assigned to. I hope they were.

XVIII

Colonel Gary Volesky handed me a baseball cap as I walked into his office.

"Just to welcome you," he said. "Because while you're here with us, you're part of the family."

It was a khaki cap bearing the insignia of the 1st Cavalry Division—a horse over a stripe—and, written on the edge of the brim, the words ARMY STRONG, CAV TOUGH. I accepted the hat with one hand and Volesky's unusually strong shake with the other. We sat down around one corner of a table. The major who had shown me in, a friendly, middle-aged African American woman named Ramona Bellard, was the Chief Public Affairs Officer, and thus responsible for coordinating embedded journalists. She sat at the other end of the table and recorded our conversation on a notepad.

Wall maps dominated Volesky's office, laying out Mosul and the surrounding areas in topographical reds and greens and grays, the Area of Operation (AO) for the United States Army's 3rd Combat Brigade, 1st Cavalry Division—Volesky's command. He was the ultimate on-site American authority, though what this meant, exactly, was up for debate. It did mean, without question, that when he wanted to fly from Mosul south along the Tigris to Qaiyara for a ceremonial transfer of power over to a Sunni militia, his helicopter left on time. It did not mean that he had the authority to tell me what everyone took for granted, knew in their steel trauma plates—that when the authority over the Sunni militias was handed from the American military to the Iraqis, the Sunni militias would be dangerous once again, because they would be paid half as much when they were being paid at all, which meant that America would no longer be buying them off.

He seemed like a knowledgeable man, however, and was well respected by everyone I spoke with in his brigade. His personal security officer, ready to take a bullet, had served under him in Sadr City in '04 and '05 and recalled that Volesky went out on patrol with his guys in the very worst of it. The only criticism I ever heard was from a warrant officer in the 1-12, who joked that he didn't understand the brigade slogan. Volesky had coined an unofficial motto, "Inject the Venom," even though the brigade's call sign was "Greywolf." It was printed on posters and T-shirts and floated, in red lettering, on computer screensavers. I never heard Volesky say it, but GIs told me that he often repeated it in passing as a kind of mini pep talk, and would chuck you on the arm, leaving you sore.

The big news the week I met him was Obama's announcement of a new plan for the American withdrawal. Several reporters had been dispatched to Mosul, which was where most of the fighting was happening at that time. The idea was to see how the best-laid plans looked in the worst place. So the obvious question for Col. Volesky, the one I suspect he fielded from every journalist who did an entrance interview that month, was "What about withdrawal?" That is, what did he think about it, what would happen when the Americans left, would all the interpreters get killed as they feared, would the insurgents take over the city completely, and *were we really going to leave?*

That was the question behind all the questions. It was hard to believe that we would, with more than four thousand servicemen dead and six hundred and fifty billion dollars spent. It seemed like too much to untangle so quickly. But Obama had said that every soldier would be out by the end of 2011, and his credibility was good then.

FOB lore had it that Volesky could out-marathon anyone in the brigade. Even as he sat, calmly, straight backed in his chair, the veins stood out on his neck, the skin was tight over his jaw, the sinews were visible in his arms. And he had great big ears, which stuck out like butterfly wings. His answers were the answers of a good soldier—non-answers. He said that he didn't think about anything except *fixing Mosul* and the welfare of his soldiers and the people of Mosul and implementing the administration's plans, and beyond that *you know as much as I do.* And to this I said, several times in different ways: *But really, are we really going to leave? Because, you know, it's still fucked up out there.*

Volesky stuck to his story. After a few minutes of trying it from different angles, I gave up. I asked him to tell me his own story instead, to leave questions of withdrawal aside, to start at the beginning.

He didn't start at the beginning, though.

"Well, first, let me say this," he said. "I was stationed in *Germany* in *1990.*" And then he dipped his chin and raised his eyebrows and looked at me silently for a full beat. There was a small smile creeping around the bottom of his tight face, as though he had said something clever, answered a question without actually saying anything at all.

XIX

What the cook thinks of the press.

6 a.m., surrounded by Iraqis, sixty-six hundred miles from Birmingham, pouring eggs out of a carton, in a trailer next to a mortar crater.

Reporter: "You're the cook, huh? That's a pretty good job, I guess. So did you want to be the cook, or how do you get that job?"

XX

In urban Iraq, electrical wires run tangled, haphazard and low over the city streets. Even labyrinths have their logic, though, and when there is any power at all the electrons get through. The MRAPs that the Americans rode around in, however, were so tall that they tore down the wires they passed beneath. In the context of the new counterinsurgency effort, this was bad news. *Bad for the relationship.* Someone devised a solution. A long, smooth, curved pole was affixed to the front of each MRAP, such that it guided any wires it ran into over the fixed protrusions of the vehicle. Sometimes it saved the wires, and this was valuable. Sometimes, though, even after the poles, locals would confront a lieutenant on foot patrol and demand an explanation. *Why must you keep tearing down the wires here?* And this particular lieutenant whom I am thinking of would apologize and promise, *We will not tear down the wires anymore.* But the MRAPs did still tear some of the wires down. If a vehicle passed in reverse, for example, the wires were simply trapped under the pole, torn off, and dragged down the street. All the drivers knew this, as did the gunners who watched the wires catch and snap at eye level, but what the fuck were they gonna do? Not reverse? Not drive fast? Not be there at all?

The lieutenant's words became more nuanced in some of the neighborhoods where his trucks had suddenly silenced so many air conditioners, interrupted so many movies. He stopped promising that the MRAPs would not tear down wires. He promised instead that he would do his best not to tear down wires. In fact, he told me, it was true of all his missions. "I never promise anything," he said. "Not anymore."

XXI

The ironies were easy: "The lack of national pride is going to be the downfall of Iraq," said one of the Americans as he stood watching the Iraqis hard at work.

In the parking lot of a joint U.S./Iraqi Combat Outpost that afternoon, IA were loading sacks of rice onto a flatbed truck. Major James Umbarger watched, rocking on his heels as he shook his head at the way the Iraqis were operating. No handoff line, no plan. It seemed like every time I saw American soldiers watch Iraqi soldiers do anything—move a detainee, take cover, set up a roll of concertina wire—the Americans complained. They talked about how the Iraqis needed to *learn to take care of themselves*, or what *dumbshits* they were, or how *corrupt* they were, or how I really ought to read this book— *what was it called?—oh yeah,* The Arab Mind, *because they really just think differently than we do.*

"Look at the way they're doing that," said Umbarger. "You know why what happened in 1776 happened? It just sort of happened. One of the biggest problems is convincing these guys to go outside the wire every day and die for the people of Mosul."

More head-shaking. It wasn't just the Americans who shook their heads, either. Blue the terp, of Kurdistan, agreed. Maybe it was because he was a Kurd and these IA were Arabs, but Blue said he didn't have a problem with Arabs. He was married to an Arab girl, in fact, a Sunni like him, of course, even though his uncles had told him that they'd find him the most beautiful girl from among his cousins.

"But hey," Blue said, over the unsteady thump of the rice sacks and generator hum. "I like this girl."

He liked her so much that he was going to try to send for her once he got to Europe. He was going to cross into Turkey, continue on to Greece, and then smuggle himself into the Netherlands. This would cost fourteen thousand U.S. dollars, he said, and he was saving his money. Blue was convinced it would be deadly for anyone who had worked with the United States to remain in Iraq after the withdrawal, and he was determined to get out by then. The Netherlands were his final destination because he knew someone there who could get him a job in a potato-chip factory.

This was an interesting story from Blue, and Umbarger and the rest were listening to it when there was a spray of gunshots somewhere outside the walls of the COP, not far away. Gunfire was common, though; the IA kept loading the trucks, and most of the Americans didn't leave the lot. A few walked into the old garage that housed the TOC to check the surveillance cameras, and I joined them. Inside, four noncoms sat at a foldout table and stared into a computer monitor displaying a checkpoint just outside the wire.

"They're so used to the cameras," said one of the noncoms, "they don't even stand up." He manipulated a small joystick, turning the picture this way and that. There was no one in the picture save a single Iraqi, sitting in a chair between blast walls, his Kalashnikov over his knees. I asked a staff sergeant if it was unusual that all of this military personnel standing around, American and Iraqi alike, should hear gunfire so close by and not move.

"Well," he said, "you gotta be careful when you react to the gunfire, so you don't enter someone else's AO. Usually we wait for a report to see if there's an immediate threat."

There didn't seem to be one. Back in the lot, another major had arrived, one Adam Lowemaster, and stood with Umbarger, watching

Iraqis load the trucks. Lowemaster was a wiry Asian American guy, even-voiced, and seemed to be Umbarger's direct superior. He was a National Police Transition Team (NPTT) leader, and his job was to train the Iraqi NP to take over when the Americans were gone. Maybe because he was in some respects a teacher, he talked about the Iraqis a little differently. You could hear the briefs he had written in his voice.

"They're very receptive to the way we target individuals," he said. The first truck was nearly full of rice. "What they are not amenable to is the way we collect intelligence. They only use sources." Now he shook his head, too. "Which means confessions."

More gunfire. This time, the guys from the platoon all ran to their trucks, and I followed, leaving Umbarger and Lowemaster behind. A sister platoon was taking small-arms fire, and we raced off the COP in the MRAPs, hopping dividers, cutting off traffic, speeding the wrong way up one-way streets. In the five minutes it took for us to get to the scene the firing stopped, and everyone calmed down after their sister platoon radioed that everyone was fine, the only casualties were two little boys, one KIA, one not.

The lieutenant colonel for the area, Ciopolla, arrived shortly after we did. "Tragedy about those little boys," he said, as we walked away from where they'd fallen.

He decided, because he was there, to say hello to the neighborhood that afternoon, and he *Salaam alaikum*-ed everyone. At one storefront he asked, "How is security?"

"Good, but the barriers are no good," said the owner. His name was Jassim. Born and raised in Mosul, his shirt and hands covered in grease, unafraid among the oil heaters he repaired and sold.

"As security improves we can take them down," said Ciopolla. "But just today we were dropping off humanitarian aid and two people tried to shoot us and killed a little boy. We went down the street to ask what had happened but no one had seen anything. The people need to help us so no more children have to die."

After our walk, Ciopolla told me that there was an irony to the mission: his men had been shot at by people they were trying to help. But there was another easy irony: if they hadn't been dropping off aid, then maybe the boy wouldn't be dead. However you looked at it, Ciopolla was proud of his men. No room for irony about that, with a lieutenant colonel.

XXII

Combat Outpost Crazy Horse was situated south of Mosul, in the desert. The American soldiers who manned it, a company of the 1st Battalion, 12th Cavalry regiment, did a lot of driving. Their battalion was responsible for fully a third of Nineveh province, and most of that was desert. The COP had a dusty, empty feel, like the desert around it. Before the war, it had been a warehouse, but no one knew for what.

Inside, on the door to a room full of jerky and refrigerated Gatorade, someone had posted a copy of the Gettysburg Address. I never saw any of the soldiers pausing to read it, though it was posted directly opposite the COP's modest Tactical Operations Center.

The Gettysburg Address was delivered on November 19, 1863, some thirteen years before General George Armstrong Custer was killed at the Battle of the Little Bighorn. The Address and Little Bighorn don't really have much to do with each other, except for being famously American. The Address didn't have much to do with the war in Iraq, either. And yet there were these connections, these ideas that haunted the desert, denied reason. Like the Iraqi journalist who told me that the United States and al Qaeda were working together. Or like the story about the Baghdad station chief doing shots off a naked woman's chest in a bar in the Green Zone. Or the Iraqi Army colonel who looked at a black American Captain from Georgia and insisted that he was Baswari. It all seemed too crazy. But there was the Gettysburg Address, hanging unread on a door in a 12th Cavalry Combat Outpost named for the man who killed the most famous commander of the 7th Cavalry.

XXIII

At breakfast outside a palace Saddam had built for one of his daugh-
ters (or cousins, maybe, none of the Americans knew, and none of the
terps were around, and there was no one to ask, though it was center
city), a sergeant talked about the way guys react to the *really bad shit.*
A litter of stray pups played with each other on a pile of garbage
bags nearby, their mother watching the soldiers carefully, waiting for
scraps. This sergeant had known guys who refused to take off their
body armor. Guys who started dragging their gun. Most guys just
handled it, of course. He knew a guy who was the only survivor in
the middle of a flatbed full of bodies, and when the truck had gotten
back to base he'd just started unloading all the bodies around him.

The sergeant described how one guy in Sadr City had taken off
all of his gear and clothing and walked out into the middle of the
street yelling, "You want me? Here I am!" The strange thing about
that, though, was that none of the soldiers ever went anywhere alone.
If that guy was on patrol, he would have had to strip before his buddies could have stopped him and tossed him in the truck. And if he
was on the Sadr City combat outpost, he would have had to sneak off
somehow, because you couldn't just go for a walk. The story didn't
really make any sense, except, of course, it did. So no one pressed the
sergeant, and then breakfast was over, and some of the soldiers tossed
their leftover eggs to the wild dogs running around the palace, and
some didn't.

XXIV

Everyone had talismans. The detail was such a cliché that I came to think of knowing what the soldiers carried for luck as a kind of reporter's talisman. A mental rabbit's foot, reassurance that you were not part of the circus, that in fact you were standing outside the tent and not responsible, somehow, for all the misunderstandings. As if, because you were not shooting, you were not as important, or as unimportant, as the GIs. I met a guy who carried a page from a little bible in a pocket on every limb.

More likely to save you than your talisman was your body armor, but lots of guys said that if it was up to them they wouldn't wear the stuff at all. No one could outrun a ball bearing, but the thinking was still that it slowed you down. It was heavy, uncomfortable. Everyone wore it, though, and there were a lot of stories about how well it worked. One was about a sergeant who was walking through a palm grove when an insurgent popped up, maybe fifteen feet ahead of him, and fired off a burst of rounds square into his chest. The sergeant went down, all the air blown out of him, but the armor stopped the rounds. His friends, not far down the road, were still lining the shooter up when the sergeant took out the insurgent from the ground. But as one corporal pointed out to me as we talked about IEDs: no body armor on your legs.

XXV

The new counterinsurgency theory called for a lot of meetings with Iraqis. The GIs called these meetings *chai-ops*, for the tea that was served. *Chai-ops* had a dismissive sense, like it wasn't real infantry work, which, of course, it wasn't. It was talking instead of patrolling, defending, fighting. And it seemed as though there were only a few things to talk about, that the jokes between Iraqis and Americans in every chai-op I ever saw were the same. They talked about family, and "How is the security situation in your area?" and "My patrol is going to go here," and money. They talked about how good the chai was.

Chai was one of the few Arabic words that the GIs used all the time. Another was *mukhtar*. The literal meaning of the word is "chosen," but they used it to describe a local leader and pronounced it *mooktar*. It was as though the lieutenants and enterprising sergeants had read the counterinsurgency manual—*build relationships with local leaders*—and then decided to go into every police station asking the chief about *mukhtars*. As though they could meet one and then check that box. Relationship built. I actually watched one police chief put his hands over his eyes when a young lieutenant, Jones, walked into his office and said to him, "So, I want to meet some *mooktars*."

Jones's translator, who went by the name Omed, had a sense of the irony of the operation. He was lanky, slow moving, quick to smile, and unusually close with Jones's top noncom, one Sergeant Rojas, who was older than most, about forty. The two of them seemed like adults around the twenty-three-year-old Jones, but Jones was in command, and that day, though Omed was reluctant to press the Iraqi police chief about the *mukhtars*, LT Jones wouldn't leave without a list. So Omed asked again, and the police chief wrote out four names and phone numbers on a slip of paper, slid it across the desk, and waited silently for LT Jones to leave.

Jones wanted to meet a *mukhtar* right then, though, and so he told Omed to ask if the police commander could spare some of his men to go on patrol to meet one of the names on the list. After Omed asked three times, the chief acquiesced and called for his assistant. Satisfied, Jones and his men waited outside, between the giant blast walls they had brought in with their cranes. After fifteen minutes, Jones was getting impatient, and just as he was about to go back inside a single IP arrived, better armed than most of his colleagues. He had a rifle *and* a pistol. "Let's go," he told Omed, in Arabic.

Outside the blast walls, Jones's platoon stretched out a standard five to ten feet apart from each other. Jones pointed to the first name the commander had given him and said to the IP, who was putting on a ski mask, "So you're gonna take us to the *mooktar*?" Omed and the IP stopped and argued for a moment before the IP turned around and ran back to the police headquarters.

"What the fuck," said Jones.

"Just wait," said Omed.

While the platoon waited, a crowd of children approached, picking through the thickets of concertina wire. The soldiers at the perimeter, having taken a knee to keep watch, were about eye level with most of them, and quickly surrounded. It was a common sight. I never saw a U.S. infantryman on a knee stand up because of the ragged kids, besieged though he might be. One of the GIs handed over a pen, starting a scuffle.

Omed was tougher with the kids than the American soldiers

were. He barked at a knot of them, as if to say *You can't fool me, I speak your language*, and then swatted one. He rolled his eyes when Jones asked him to ask the kids where they lived and why they weren't in school.

The leader of the kids wasn't the biggest, but he was the most aggressive, and he had gotten the pen. He waved his hand dismissively in the direction of the buildings across the street.

"He says he lives over there," said Omed, dragging on a cigarette, "and that he is in school." One of the kids, when he saw Omed light up, produced a cigarette and lit up himself.

The IP finally returned, and the platoon set off along the deserted road toward the first *mukhtar* on the list. The house was close by, at the top of a hill overlooking the police station, and large. The GIs took knees around the entrance, and the children, who had followed, lounged on each other, watching while Omed rapped on the gate.

A boy, not much older than the street kids, maybe thirteen, opened the gate and looked nervously at Jones and Rojas, who were standing on either side of Omed. He said that his father was not home, that he was in Baghdad. Rojas told Omed to tell the kid that it wasn't for anything bad, his father wasn't in any trouble. As if they could somehow take back that they had knocked on the door, heavily armed. Jones shook his head and took out the list the police chief had given him. He called the IP over and pointed to the next name on the list. Once again the IP didn't want to go, and once again Jones insisted. The platoon set off again, deeper into the city, and this time the children disappeared. The IP pulled his mask close up over his nose.

The alleys narrowed. And then, a mile from the base, the life of the town was visible on the street. Women called their children back behind their robes as we passed. Men looked up from construction and followed us.

Along a clean, shady street, the IP indicated for us to stop, and then to follow him. He stepped quickly out of view, into a stone doorway. Rojas, Jones, and Omed followed, and the GIs set up security outside.

Two armed men in civilian clothes greeted the IP and Omed just inside, as though expecting our arrival. They gestured us into a plain sitting room, hot light seeping in from covered windows on the street, and stood at the door, smoking. As we waited, Rojas watched them, and a boy brought in a tray of sugary chai. Omed sipped and told Jones that the *mukhtar* of this house had had a good reputation with the American company on the previous deployment.

He walked in suddenly, with the air of a man who was accustomed to being listened to. Blazer, white keffiyeh, white ankle-length dishdasha, long blue socks, shined brown loafers. Everyone rose, and the greetings went on for a long time. Omed looked at Jones when they had all finally settled down, as if to say, *So what do you want to talk about?* Jones proceeded to thank the *mukhtar* again, and then suggested that they could work together. He said in particular that if the *mukhtar* knew of any weapons caches, or any bad guys, or anything like that, maybe he could talk about them. Everyone wanted to find a weapons cache.

"Because we want to be your friend," said Jones for the fifth time.

The *mukhtar* finally interrupted him, cutting off Omed as he translated.

"He says, 'Don't keep saying we want to be friends. We are friends.'"

Jones seemed lost. Rojas suggested to Omed that he ask how the *mukhtar* was doing, how his neighborhood and his family were faring. The *mukhtar* then told a long story, revealing that he had been shot and that two of his sons had been detained by the coalition. One had been released, but one was still in. He spoke at an even tempo throughout. When he finished he suggested that they all look at a map together.

"Wait," Rojas interrupted. "We have to ask him about his son."

"Yes," said Omed, and then, translating for the *mukhtar*, "'I am the only one who gives good information to the coalition. The day after they took my son, I went to the marines and a girl from the CIA said they took him to Basra. That was seven months ago.'"

"Why didn't you tell anyone about your son?" asked Rojas.

"'I was so pissed off. That's why I didn't tell anyone,'" Omed translated. "'I invite generals to my house for lunch—beef—I spend a half million dinars. All have pictures of my house, everyone knows me. Why would I work with terrorists? If they prove my son is a terrorist, I don't care, kill him. A major promised he would see what happened, but he has done shit. They came with helicopters and dogs. The Colonel told me show anyone this paper and they will respect you.'"

The *mukhtar* produced a sheet of paper from within his blazer. It read:

26 April, 2005

Memo for Record

Subject: West Tigris River Valley Leader Identification

Khames Mahmood Jasem was a *mukhtar* in Hamam al Alil... He has expressed a desire to Coalition Forces to improve the security situation. He assisted the Coalition by identifying at least 3 IED. The COA endorses these desires.

Todd B. McCaffrey

LTC in Command

Rojas and Jones looked at the paper and handed it back.

"The problem with that is that was a different unit," said Jones, shrugging. "We're new—"

"'The Coalition put me in jail for ten days. You know how I got out? When they were searching my laptop they saw a picture of me with a coalition general and then they let me go.'" The *mukhtar* collected himself, paused. "'I want to know who gave you info about my son,'" he said.

Jones promised he would look into it. Now that they had been talking for a while, he seemed more at ease, as though the mission was going well. He radioed for one his guys outside to bring in a satellite map, and asked if the *mukhtar* could show him a few things.

"This thing about his son is important," said Rojas, as they were spreading out the map on the thinly carpeted floor.

The *mukhtar* quietly described populations and a few of the boundaries everyone who lived there knew. Jones and Rojas drew behind his dark finger in grease pencil, and then Rojas carefully folded the map and tucked it into one of his pockets, as though he had acquired something of great value.

"Okay," said Jones. "Thank him and all that stuff."

"Tell him we will look into his son," said Rojas.

Omed did, but as we all stood up the *mukhtar* put his hand on Jones's shoulder and looked him right in the eyes and spoke. To his right, in the sunlight creeping through the curtains, reflecting off the sticky, empty teacups, Omed said for the *mukhtar*, "'Iraqi police chief Halid is a bad guy, and is still working with bad guys.'"

The *mukhtar* took his hand from the lieutenant's shoulder and nodded his head again, solemnly confirming the translator's words, which he could not understand but seemed to have faith in.

"Who is Halid?" Jones said to Rojas.

"The guy with thirty IPs outside his house."

The *mukhtar* spoke again and Omed translated, "'If you search his house, I'm sure you will find something—'"

Jones cut him off. "It's just not that easy," he said, raising his hands.

"'—see how many guys he kills in Mosul,'" continued Omed for the *mukhtar*.

"We can't just go into houses," Jones protested, "we need to work with the IP on everything—"

But now Omed cut *him* off. "I don't want to tell him this stuff," he said.

And then Omed said his own goodbye and thank you and was the first one out the door. Jones followed, and outside he took out the list of *mukhtars* from his pocket.

"That's enough for today," he said, looking at the list.

*U.S. infantrymen oversee the distribution of sacks of rice by Iraqi Army, west Mosul,
on the afternoon the little boy was killed in the crossfire by insurgents.*

The view across Mosul from Bash Tapia Castle, along the Tigris River.

Foot patrol through the alleys of Ras al-Khor, shortly before a grenade attack on LT Kim and his platoon, west Mosul.

Men of A Company in the
3-8 Cavalry who patrolled Ras al-Khor.

TOP ROW:
Private First Class (PFC) Ricky Cotton
and PFC Erik Papocchia.

MIDDLE ROW:
Specialist (SPC) Ratu Mawi
and SPC Zach Holmberg.

LEFT:
1st Lieutenant Richard Kim.

Mine-Resistant Ambush-Protected vehicles (MRAPS) parked inside the wire at Combat Outpost Courage, central Mosul.

An Iraqi contractor accepting payment from the U.S. Army civil-affairs squad, inside an MRAP, east Mosul.

Mosaic of Saddam Hussein inside Combat Outpost Courage, formerly one of his palaces, central Mosul.

U.S. and Iraqi Army foot patrol, Mahmour, southeast Mosul.

The back of an open MRAP.

Census mission in south Mosul. The kind of nighttime door-knocking that Gu was particularly good at.

Iraqi soldier keeping warm, west Mosul.

Ceremony marking the transfer of authority over the Sons of Iraq security forces from the U.S. to the Iraqi government, south Mosul.

Breakfast at Combat Outpost Courage.

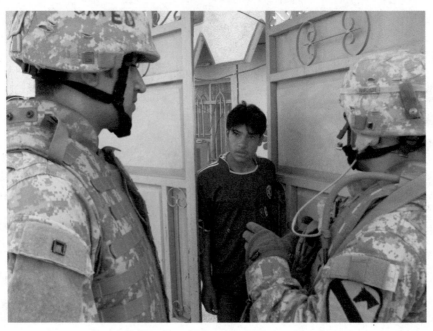

Chai-ops: looking for mukhtars with LT Jones and his platoon.

Wreckage of car bomb, Iraqi police checkpoint, west Mosul.

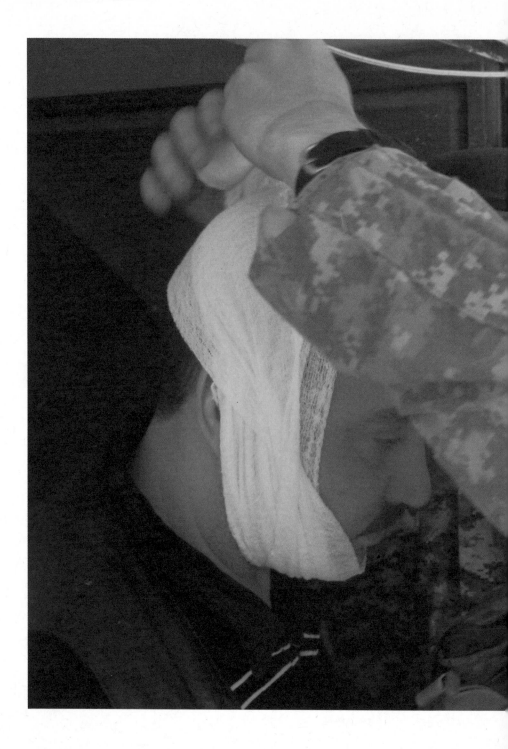

SPC Adam Gade, a medic, treats a detainee at an Iraqi police station in west Mosul.

The windshield of LT Kim's humvee. He and some of the men in his platoon picked the verse together.

On patrol the afternoon the little boys were hit in the crossfire, west Mosul.

XXVI

Occasionally, dust storms turned the air thick and golden, but the soldiers never remarked on the particle beauty. There were a lot of things like that, phenomena of war and occupation that seemed gorgeous inside their awful frames. Of course, the dust storm was really a phenomenon of the natural world, but everything seemed like it was part of the occupation.

A common complaint among the officers and enlisted men both was that they were doing a job they had never been trained to do. They were infantry soldiers, trained to kill people and destroy a country, and they were being ordered to do the opposite. The rules of engagement were different in the beginning, the veterans might reminisce as they bounced along a street that had suffered *only two* IED explosions that week. *Yeah, it was different when you could just open up on 'em. Not the same anymore.*

Not all of the changes that brought the level of violence down were as simple as reconfiguring the rules of engagement. The Surge, for example, was partly about an increase in troop levels. But it was also about delivering suitcases full of American dollars in vacuum-sealed plastic bags to Sunni sheiks so that they would not fight the occupiers anymore. So that they might even help the occupiers with the truest crazy assholes, the radical al Qaeda ideologues who wouldn't be bribed. It was true that the United States does not negotiate with terrorists; if you demanded the removal of American forces from the holy Arabian Peninsula and threatened to kill Bo, the new First Dog, then the United States would not talk with you. But the United States did buy off much of the Sunni insurgency; it negotiated with terrorist networks. And the week of the fifth anniversary of the battle for Fallujah, Navy Seals killed three Somali pirates holding a hostage, and, between B-rolls of the Gulf of Aden, the presidential Portuguese Water Dog received near constant television coverage.

XXVII

Another parking lot, more waiting around. Sometimes it seemed like the whole war was spent waiting to get inside an armored vehicle that sat like a big dumb animal on the dirt lot in front of some empty warehouse or palace or school or whatever it had been before, who gave a shit, now it was a COP. You were waiting in a parking lot. No wonder it seemed like so many of the soldiers didn't know anything about Iraqis. They knew what they knew from hanging around parking lots. Which was what a lot of the U.S. soldiers liked to do back home anyway.

But not Specialist Patterson, twenty-seven, of Western Pennsylvania. Waiting and smoking there in that particular dirt lot—COP Courage—he told me he liked the countryside. A medic with the 1-12 Cav in Mosul, and circumspect, like many medics, Patterson was thin, pale, quiet, steady. Freckles smeared his sharp features. He was popular and, of course, nicknamed Doc. He seemed like a leader, the way that some guys just did when others didn't. The captain of that particular company, Sucec, didn't have the same carriage; you could tell from the way his head swiveled around as he walked up on us that morning. Sucec offered me a cigar and we walked a lap around the parking lot while Patterson and his guys watched us. The city was much improved, Sucec told me, better every day. It was hard to take him seriously. He was relentlessly earnest about the occupation, and he never smiled. When we were done with our lap we stood in front of Patterson and the juniors and noncoms again and Sucec said something to me about how the soldiers could say all kinds of crazy stuff, and I should "take it with a grain of salt." Then he walked off, leaving me with his men. No one said anything as he walked away, or even after he was out of earshot.

It had been a strange week. For the first time in over a month, a mortar had landed on the FOB, killing a private in logistics, a supply clerk, a woman. Patterson and company had not been able to check their email or make any phone calls because of the casualty. Whenever a U.S. servicemember is killed in action there's a base-wide blackout so that the identity of the casualty doesn't leak off the base before the responsible casualty-notification officer can inform the family. And meanwhile Patterson and his buddies had to wear their body armor and gear on the FOB, because intelligence said there were continuing mortar threats. *Sucks to have to wear your Kevlar to the DFAC*. And even though the platoon sent out to get the assholes who did it had found the mortar tubes they'd used on the back of a pickup truck not that far outside the wire, there was no one to kill and nothing to blow up because the truck had already been all fucked up by the mortars launching out of the cab—*fuckin dumb hajji*—and whoever had fired them was long since gone. And that sucked too. Neither Patterson nor his squad sergeant nor any of the guys in his truck had known the woman who had been killed. Her battalion commander told me that she'd weighed one hundred pounds.

So Patterson and his buddies were happy to be off the FOB, standing there smoking in the dirt parking lot of COP Courage, because on the COP it was just them and their lieutenant, except when Sucec showed up. Their schedule was harder out there but they still liked it better. *Just us*. Counterinsurgency doctrine called for breaking patterns (and understanding those of your enemy), so three times a month they were based on the COP for quick-reaction force shift, or QREF, free to patrol at their LT's discretion but usually just waiting, listening to the radio. If anyone else in sector got into trouble, Patterson and his platoon dropped the PlayStation controls or the dumbbells and roared out to help. Usually, by the time they got there, whatever had happened was over. Most of the incidents at this point in the war were IED explosions or lobbed grenades, not pin-down firefights, so it was almost impossible for a quick-reaction force to be quick enough. But then, sometimes one incident incited another. A favored technique of IED planters was to lay a second charge, so that when a squad arrived to evacuate the wounded and secure the area they would get blown up, too. This strategy was of particular consequence to medics. *One incident or two? One Gulf War or two?*

It wasn't like the Crusades, for example, in which there was no confusion about when and where the battles began and ended, even a thousand years later. On the last Tuesday in November, 1095, Pope Urban II told a crowd of French Christians that "A race absolutely alien to God has invaded the land of Christians, has reduced the people with sword, rapine, and flame." And the battle began. Eventually the Christians even made it to Mosul, to the same streets where Patterson's job was to pull ball bearings out of kids from Colorado. *Gesta Francorum et aliorum Hierosolimitanorum*, or "The deeds of the Franks and the other Pilgrims to Jerusalem," is a Latin account of the First Crusade, in which you can find this description of Mosul's ruler at the time:

> Kerbogha had with him a great army whom he had been assembling for a long time, and had been given leave by the khalif who is the pope of the Turks, to kill Christians... [He had] collected an immense force of pagans—Turks, Arabs, Saracens, Paulicians, Azymites, Kurds, Persians, Agulani, and many other people who could not be counted.

Kerbogha, presumably, had not shaken hands with Urban the decade before, like Saddam had shaken hands with Rumsfeld. But even then, it seems, the city was filled with foreign men determined to fight the occupiers. Maybe in 3010 the dozen creeping IED cells will be as clearly delineated as Saracens, Azymites, Paulicians. Omar al-Baghdadi's men might be so listed, have parts of the country named after them. Like Specialist Patterson's part of the world, divided into the names of men who lived there a long time ago: Jacksonville, Dallas, Seattle.

"So is it getting a lot better?" I asked, lamely, breaking the silence Sucec had left us in.

More silence against the generator background. Then Patterson sort of chuckled and shook his head. "They were fighting each other before we got here," he said. "They're gonna be fighting after we leave."

"Fuckin' Sucec," I heard someone mutter, as we mounted up.

XXVIII

Forward Operating Base Marez was like a small town. There were busy intersections, commuters, a Burger King, a couple of coffee shops, a PX (Post Exchange) which resembled a Kmart. There was even a barbershop called Pop's and Omar's across from the DFAC, next to the soccer field. The soccer field was rarely used by the Americans, but the Filipinos and Indians and Sri Lankans and Peruvians loved it, and played in some combination almost every night, after they were finished scooping ice cream at the dessert bar in the DFAC or driving ten thousand gallons of used toilet water from one end of the base to the other. Where exactly that water went was unclear—every day you would see the great big white trucks with NON POTABLE WATER printed on them sucking out the toilet trailers and driving off to some other part of the base. But then where exactly the Southeast Asians went was unclear, too.

"Fuckin' fobbits," one Sergeant told me dismissively. "Who knows what they really do."

Fobbit: someone who never went off base. (I heard someone at Marez describe them as "small furry faggots, like in the *Lord of the Rings* movies.") Like the logistics private who had been killed that week, or the Ugandan contractors who worked security at the dining facility, or even the Iraqis who lived on the FOB because the walls had literally risen up around them. Many of those Iraqis had fled or been killed, but the ones that stayed and got clearance became part of the place.

Pop's and Omar's was like that. It had been annexed by the FOB.

Inside, a row of chairs along a mirrored wall was always full. There was actually a lot of room for styling within the framework of Army-standard haircuts, though some GIs said that they didn't give a shit what they looked like out here and just shaved it all off. Still, whenever I heard someone say something like this it reminded me of the quiet of Pop's and Omar's. Iraqis snipping away and soldiers reading *Stars and Stripes* and quietly chatting about flattops and fades and jarheads and sideburns of various lengths and shapes.

The spec ops guys were held in particularly high regard, because they could dress like civilians and were said to be allowed to have any facial hair they wanted. It turned out that this wasn't entirely true. One of them explained to me that it was only a month into his deployment (*really quiet, we only killed like twenty-five guys*) that his company was permitted to grow beards. So they had their own rules, too.

XXIX

It was common knowledge among the GIs that every Iraqi household was entitled, under Iraqi law, to an AK-47 assault rifle and a single magazine. The guys who understood this best were men like Staff Sergeant David Kelley, a sergeant from Cheyenne Wells, Colorado, population 1,010.

"Like me," he said. He didn't really *need* assault rifles back home, but he liked having them. The Iraqis didn't *need* their AKs either, really, but then what would they fire at weddings?

Kelley was very tall, pushing 6'6", but he didn't mind riding in the hot, cramped darkness of a Bradley. There was a screen on which you could see a gray, glowing rectangle of the outside world, but the overwhelming sensation of the vehicle was of pressure and darkness, like being on the inside of a grenade that was about to detonate. And then the back hatch would drop and the GIs would dismount as quickly as they could, blinking out in the dusty sun. The problem with using a Bradley in Mosul was that they were too big. They couldn't make turns in the narrow streets, or even fit at all, sometimes. So we usually parked outside the labyrinth and the men went in on their feet. The old and sacred contradiction. They were about to take fire, or an IED, or a grenade, but they walked into the alleys anyway. You could see the apprehension in some of the GIs every time, but in others, like Kelley, you never did. He walked with the same gait and talked in the same flat, Western voice all the time, unfolding mantis-like from a Bradley or walking into those alleys.

At the COP one evening, I sat with Kelley while he unrolled his hammock and hung it up between HESCO baskets behind the bunk trailer. His hammock was the envy of the several other guys in the platoon, guys who slept out there with him on cots or on the ground. But even the ground was better than the trailer. Inside, the bunk beds were packed so closely together that if you rolled over you'd end up in the next guy's bed—or, in the free-floating homo-erotic shit-talking vernacular, with your cock in somebody's mouth.

Kelley, home-schooled and quiet, wasn't given to that kind of shit-talking. He had lost several buddies on his previous tour in Baqubah and had a kind of sadness about him, like he was resigned to staying in Iraq for a long time, even if it wasn't with the U.S. Army.

His contract was up after this tour, but he was trying to stay in Iraq as a security contractor. All his gear was his own except for his gun, he said, sipping on an energy drink beside his hammock in the fading light of the afternoon.

"And besides, what else would I do?"

Maybe he was right. Certainly he had his job figured out. A couple weeks after that, a mortar dropped through the trailer. It didn't kill anyone, didn't even detonate, but it destroyed the bunk beds and some kit. Not Kelley's hammock, though.

XXX

It was not a war in which you often had to run. Many of the soldiers were overweight. One of the heaviest I knew was Smoke, though under his armor there seemed to be as much strength as fat. He walked around the base slowly, drawling and stately on his way to the MRAPs at dawn, his yellow reflection sash shining across his shoulder and belly like the tape cyclists put on their helmets. Everyone was supposed to wear the sashes so that they didn't get hit by the trucks that were always zooming along the base's muddy roads. Smoke didn't get out of anyone's way.

He dipped, like many of the young men there, and carried an empty plastic bottle to spit his juice into. He only removed the wad of tobacco from his lip on his way into the DFAC, as he passed by the Ugandans not checking IDs at the final checkpoint inside the great concrete T-walls. If you asked Smoke if he thought it was strange that Ugandans were standing guard while he ate two bacon cheeseburgers between patrols in a city most of his countrymen had never heard of, he would tell you something like "I don't talk politics. I'm just here to serve."

Smoke didn't know, exactly, where his name came from. None of the sergeants on Forward Operating Base Diamondback did; it was an old Army nickname that tracked from war to war. The best guess was that it originated during the Civil War, when cannon-platoon sergeants would be obscured by the clouds of smoke belched from their guns. Another idea was that the *Smoke* was the guy who lit the fuses.

Smoke referred my question to Top, the first sergeant of his company. Top was an institutional name too, of course, and a sign of respect derived from the first sergeant's position as the highest-ranking enlisted man in the company. Just like there were plenty of Smokes in the Army, there were plenty of Tops. Smoke was convinced, however, that his Top was "the best," and liked talking about him. When I thanked Smoke for taking me around with him and introducing me to some of his men, he said that since Top had asked him to do it, that's what he was going to do. It was a statement about discipline and orders, but he said it almost affectionately. He told me I didn't have to thank him.

"You could really learn a thing or two from Top," Smoke said, spitting into his bottle for emphasis as we tramped through the mud back toward Top's quarters after dinner.

Top looked like an older version of Smoke, pale and deeply Southern. They both came from families of enlisted men, and it was not hard to imagine generations of Smokes and Tops confiding in each other, new fathers and sons in theater, old fathers and sons at home. Smoke had one child, and Top had three, mostly grown. That night we found Top sitting on the wooden railing outside of Company B's TOC, spitting tobacco into a plastic bottle. Top lived with the officers, but he was only around a corner of T-wall from his enlisted men. He pointed this out to me as Smoke strolled off, relieved of reporter duty.

"So," said Top, "how was dinner with the real Army?"

"Good," I said. "Smoke's a good guy."

"Do you play chess?" he asked me.

Top had a chess set in his Army-clean room. The board was large, and the metal pieces were comic-book Persian, romantic. The gold queen was buxom and wore a veil. The silver king sported a long beard. Top told me that he had received the set as a gift from a Kurdish friend who ran a café not far from the base.

"I bet you were wondering how we got stuff," he said, smirking. "Well, ask anyone, they'll tell you Top knows how to get stuff."

As we set up the pieces, Top bragged about his relationship with the Kurd who gave him the board. He told me about meals various Kurds had cooked for him, and how whenever he needed to get off base he could go over to their place for a hookah smoke. "And you know what? The food's not even that bad."

As we played he asked me, obliquely, what Smoke had said that evening. We hadn't talked about anything but the food, really. I had listened as Smoke talked with some of his buddies about other guys they knew. But Top seemed concerned that I would write his men up in a poor light. He excused them, said they were good men but they said stupid shit sometimes.

We played three games and Top won the last two.

"Good to play chess with you," he said. We shook hands. We were buddies. "Go easy on my guys," he told me.

"I'm not here to nail anyone," I said.

I thought about the chess games a few days later when I was passing through the Battalion TOC. I noticed Smoke waiting outside an office door with several of the guys in his squad, cleaned up and nervous. Smoke and I nodded at each other. Down the hall, I asked the public-affairs officer I was meeting what was up. He said he didn't know, but that it was a drug thing. Someone had been caught buying from the Kurds off the base, he'd heard, some heroin thing.

"It's amazing what those Kurds can get," he told me.

XXXI

Everyone lay in bed the same way. Smoke, for example, had the bed closest to the door and a free top bunk, which he had turned into a sort of mini chow-hall staging area. He had an array of sugary cereals up there, and the brightly colored boxes contrasted sharply with the camo of the rest of the quarters. Smoke's normal state of repose involved leaning on an elbow and looking into the laptop that he had resting on a trunk at eye level. I saw soldiers in this position every time I went into their living quarters: in bed, Skyping or Gchatting with their wives and girlfriends and families and buddies back home. In bed, thousands of miles away. At least, that's how it was for the grunts who had laptops.

XXXII

Those two little boys who got shot. I spoke with the company commander afterward, Captain Ferguson. According to his guys, one block from Zanjali Traffic Circle two masked men dressed in black had stepped from behind a corner and fired Kalashnikovs at one of the platoon's MRAPs, pumping rounds into the armor of the vehicle and the flesh of two little boys who happened to be in the way. While Ferguson and I and his translator, Blue, were talking about this at the edge of the traffic circle, a trio of children were leaning on each other nearby, gawking at the American soldiers who had set up a perimeter around us to interview witnesses.

Pointing at the three kids, I asked Captain Ferguson if he thought they might know the two boys who had been shot. Ferguson told Blue to ask them. Blue called them over, asking first where they were from, and about school, and then about the shootings. They smiled coyly and said they didn't know anything about it. I mentioned to Captain Ferguson how remarkable I found this, that the kids seemed to be playing happily in the same street where one of their peers had died, with tanks and gun-toting men all around.

"Nah, they're not afraid of the rifles," he told me. "But look at this."

Captain Ferguson casually drew his pistol, pointing it at the ground. The children turned and ran as fast as they could.

"What happened?" I asked.

Captain Ferguson told me that he had seen it all over. Kids would reach out to touch M4s, had no fear of Kalashnikovs, would scurry before an oncoming Bradley and run behind a Humvee or wave all day to nervous chain-smoking soldiers at a thrice-bombed checkpoint. But if they saw a pistol, they would run. The reason, he said, was that in Saddam's time only the elite were allowed to carry pistols. They were considered glamorous, and favored for executions. Anytime a man produced a pistol, the likelihood of a shooting increased dramatically. The children remembered, he told me.

"But they were hardly born before the war," I said. "How could they know?"

At the far corner of the block, the three children were staring at us as we spoke.

"They just do," Captain Ferguson told me, holstering his gun.

Then, perhaps three streets away, there was a loud boom. I jumped, and Ferguson grinned at me. "You all right?" he said, and chuckled at my nerves.

In the name of Allah, the Beneficent, the Merciful
Nay! I swear by this city.
And you shall be made free from obligation in this city—
And the begetter and whom he begot.
Certainly We have created man to be in distress.
Does he think that no one has power over him?
He shall say: I have wasted much wealth.
Does he think that no one sees him?
Have We not given him two eyes,
And a tongue and two lips,
And pointed out to him the two conspicuous ways?
But he would not attempt the uphill road,
And what will make you comprehend what the uphill road is?
(It is) the setting free of a slave,
Or the giving of food in a day of hunger
To an orphan, having relationship,

Or to the poor man lying in the dust.

Then he is of those who believe and charge one another to show patience,
and charge one another to show compassion.

These are the people of the right hand.

And those who disbelieve in our communications, they are the people of
the left hand.

On them is fire closed over.

—Chapter 90, The Qur'an

XXXIII

Ricky was a terp who chain-smoked and always carried several packs of cigarettes. He was generous with his smokes, would shake one out for you each time you reached for your pack. His hands shook when he offered you one, though; Ricky seemed sometimes like he wanted something back. The guys he rode with liked him. He was a source of fun because of his nerves, but he played along with the jokes.

The strangest thing about Ricky was the way he perspired. The guys in the truck agreed that they had never seen anything like it. Ricky dripped. His hair was always damp. When he turned his head quickly, the saltwater sprayed off him. The canvas of his seat in the MRAP was always stained.

Ricky, like most terps, rotated between his company's platoons, but recently everyone in the 1-12's Bull company had been seeing more of him than usual. He had moved onto the FOB full time. In fact, he was living on a cot outside one of the lieutenant's rooms. This particular LT, Drew Masone, was a broad twenty-three-year-old from Levittown, Long Island, distinguished most clearly by his tolerant nature. He only shook his head about Ricky, didn't say that he was stinking up the hallway even though he was, lying on his cot in his undershirt whenever he wasn't standing outside, smoking, saying hello too many times.

Most terps went home every couple of weeks. There was, sometimes, joking between them and the soldiers about how the terps could go home and get laid and have a beer up in Kurdistan. The platoons rotated the fortnightly "terp drop," a boring and simple mission. The terps left their camo behind and piled into the back of the MRAP, often with a small refrigerator or television set or bag of clothes that they had procured in the previous two weeks of patrols. Then the patrol mounted up and drove north to a deserted stretch of road in Kurdistan where a couple of beat-up sedans idled. The terps would quickly dismount and load their stuff into the sedans and speed off down the road. Terp drop was easy and tedious for the GIs, but for the terps it was more important than almost anything else. It was transit between worlds. What if the wrong person saw them? What if they were followed? What if they brought the mayhem and killing back home?

Ricky, though, told me he wasn't afraid of dying. Maybe living on the base was the final move in his private cosmology of courage. He said he hated Saddam, and he was frank about his very Kurdish attitude toward the United States, which was if you were going to fight a war you should join the side that's going to win.

His brother felt the same way; he was a member of the Asayesh, the Kurdish Intelligence and Security force. The Asayesh had fought Saddam even before he'd killed close to one hundred thousand Kurds in the Al-Anfal Campaign of 1987 and '88, before George Herbert Walker Bush's administration suggested that America would support the revolution from the air in 1991. Before the gas that came when we didn't.

The Asayesh has itself been condemned by Amnesty International for human rights abuses, occasionally. If Ricky had mixed feelings about his brother's organization, he didn't let on. He only pulled up his damp shirt and showed me the ugly pink scars on his arms, and his back, and his neck.

"Saddam's army tortured me because my brother was Asayesh," he told me on our first afternoon together, in the back of an MRAP. This was news to the guys we were riding with that day, Ricky's platoon.

XXXIV

There was a lot of graffiti in Mosul, and I always asked whatever terp I was with what it said as we passed by. I always got the same answers: "God Is Great" or "For Sale."

XXXV

One battalion commander told me that the Yazidis, a Kurdish ethnic group, worshipped the Devil. They believed that they knew the spot where he had crashed to earth. The place he was referring to was Lalish, the ancient Yazidi valley settlement some sixty clicks northwest of Mosul. Lalish, according to the Yazidis, is the final resting place of Şêx Adî, the reincarnation of their creator god Tawûsê Melek, more commonly known as Lucifer. The Yazidis, the commander said, believe Lucifer was redeemed after the fall, and that he then created the universe. They think the Devil is coming back, the commander told me, laughing, leaning back in his chair in the TOC as he clicked to another slide in his PowerPoint presentation, more boxes and lines depicting how the U.S. military should understand and interact with Iraq.

Who knew what Lucifer would do if he did come back? If he looked as he did in Dante he would be enormously tall and have three heads. For him to arrive in Mosul he would have already broken free of the bottom circle of Hell, where he was frozen in place; he would have spit out Judas and Brutus and Cassius, leaving his three mouths free to tear apart the translators, who all feared that they would be the first to go. He would step over the wire of the FOB and with his cracked hands hurl the humvees upon the city, his aim perfect, divine, such that the victors landed exactly on the teenagers as they laid IEDs, thereby destroying both.

XXXVI

For God so loved the world, that He gave His one and only Son, and who-ever believes in Him shall not perish, but have eternal life. John 3:16.

This was written in black ink on the inside of the windshield of the humvee commanded by 1st Lieutenant Richard Kim, twenty-four, of the Chicago suburbs. Kim was not a particularly religious young man, but he had written the verse there the day one of his soldiers was injured by a grenade while they were on mounted patrol in west Mosul.

"I just figured, why not, you know?" he said of the inscription. He seemed almost embarrassed about it, although he told me later he was not. The verse ran along the bottom right corner of the wind-shield; above it Kim had scrawled coordinates and phone numbers when he needed to, so there were smudges and random numbers and the effect of the whole bulletproof glass canvas was hieroglyphic, particularly from the outside looking in. For most Iraqis it was all incomprehensible, backward or no.

Kim was an optimist. He called Iraq a shithole in solidarity with his men, but in quieter moments he reflected on the parts of the country that he liked. He didn't want to live there, of course, but he noticed that the houses he was running by after an explosion in the narrow alleys of Ras al-Khor were older than anything in Chicago. It was not lost on him that he was breaking down three-hundred-year-old doors.

Kim even had a couple of places that he genuinely liked in the country. His favorite was probably Bash Tapia Castle, on the banks of the Tigris in his sector of Mosul. It looked deserted, but wasn't. Around the base of the building a small maze of ruined walls sheltered nothing but trash, but at the top of the castle's tower the Iraqi Army had stationed a handful of soldiers. Kim had patrolled up there before, but the Iraqi soldiers were new and surprised to see him, or anyone, climbing up through the ruins. Kim and his sergeants waved and yelled from afar—they didn't want any misunderstandings. It's hard to mistake an American patrol—they have the cleanest, biggest, best-armed cars in the city—but still. The Iraqis on top of the castle had probably been watching Kim and his trucks drive past the Saturday congregation crowded outside the mosque across the street.

"Shit," said Kim, as old men bent down to the side of the road, toward the wall of the mosque, like tall grass. "We shouldn't have driven through this way."

If the IA on the castle had mistaken the Americans for enemies and fired from their high ground, they probably would have killed a few of them. But they would have been very lucky to escape with their own lives, after that.

One pair of IA standing guard were talkative, through a translator. A slight youth and a creased man old enough to be his grandfather. They were the same rank, and agreed that the castle was very important, but they didn't want to guard it anymore. "Iraq has been in one thousand wars," said the youth, staring down the river. He looked for a moment like he was thinking about jumping. Then he said that as soon as the Americans left, he and everyone in the Iraqi Army would take off their uniforms and run. He pointed at the ground to show where he would leave the pile of clothing. The grandfather soldier made a thumbs-up sign at the second-generation Korean lieutenant from Chicago, inker of old verses on the inside of a new humvee.

XXXVII

Eight hours off between patrols:

Of course we like war movies. We're in *a fucking war.*

XXXVIII

The guys who had their own gear had a whole industry at their service. They supplemented the standard-issue kit with GPS devices, superpowered scopes, iPhone machine-gun systems. The word for a GI who had a lot of custom kit was *geardo*, and this could become a nickname. There was one lieutenant from Arizona on his first tour who got called Geardo. Lad mags and knife catalogues and goggles and Kevlar littered the room he shared with another lieutenant.

Those catalogues, the tech—it all dictated tactics. Americans liked moving at night because of night vision, the remarkable clarity with which they could see through the darkness of a foreign city under curfew. It was counterintuitive and spooky, but that was the whole point of the Army: to train you against your instincts. Move at night, walk down that alley. The equipment seemed supernatural sometimes.

It wasn't, of course. And it became familiar, seven years into the war. You could see in a guy who had been detained enough times that he was no longer surprised by the *Hajj Box*—a retina scanner about the size and shape of a large-format camera. He would roll his eyes as Americans tried to scan him again. Some Iraqis looked like they knew how to use the box better than the Americans did; the grunts were constantly cursing it for its false positives and multiple matches. And the Hajj Box wasn't a piece of gear that the Iraqis dealt with often, if they could help it. What they dealt with all the time was the lower-tech gear that hung from every American like fruit. Gloves, clips, guns, shades. A lot of guys complained about the way Iraqis, especially Iraqi Army, would come up to them and point at some piece of kit to indicate that they wanted it. The Americans imitated the Iraqis who did this, putting on accents that didn't make any sense, cartoon Italian as much as Iraqi.

"'Meester, Meester.' Like I'm just going to give 'em a fucking grenade."

"Or my fucking sunglasses."

"Fucking retarded."

"I'll give 'em a pen sometimes."

The articulated mission at that point was to provide support for the Iraqi Army, but this did not extend to handing over gear. Especially custom gear. Arizona Geardo's prize piece of kit was his knife. A former spec ops guy, retired and living in Cairo, made the best knives in the world, Geardo told me, if you knew what to ask for.

"Who the fuck knows why he moved to Cairo," said Geardo as he unsheathed the knife. It was about twelve inches long, black, and curved like the haunches of a rabbit. On its wide spine there was an inscription: DEATH TO AL QAEDA.

XXXIX

In the parlance of the U.S. Army, a hand-grenade explosion was a "significant act." Likewise small-arms fire, improvised explosive device detonation, car bombs—all were significant acts. The daily number of significant acts—or "sig acts," as the soldiers called them—was sometimes used as a measure of progress or regression in the counterinsurgency effort. The definition of a sig act, however, was not fixed. According to some soldiers, a sig act today (one without fatalities, say) would never have been counted as one a year or two before. And so the value of the statistic was a matter of contention, even on the record, and even among battalion commanders. The lieutenant colonel responsible for East Mosul said it was an excellent metric for progress. His counterpart in West Mosul said the opposite.

The neighborhood in Mosul (and Iraq) that likely had the most sig acts per day while I was there was Ras al-Khor. It was also Mosul's oldest neighborhood. On a clear afternoon a day before the Prophet Mohammed's 1,439th birthday, I walked with LT Kim's infantry platoon from one end of it to the other.

"It's like clockwork," said Kim, as we were dismounting. He had told me that he had always wanted to be a soldier, but that afternoon he looked unhappy. "Twenty-five to thirty minutes after we get here, they'll come after us."

He was right. After thirty minutes of walking through the uneven sepia alleys of Ras al-Khor, a grenade bounced up behind the rear guard and exploded perhaps ten meters from the closest man. No one was hurt. The platoon opened fire, giving chase through the smoke.

The GI who had been closest to the explosion, Specialist Ratu Waqa Mawi, twenty-six, called "Maui Wowy" by his friends, of Fiji but waiting to be naturalized as a U.S. citizen, jabbed his gun at a large stone house. "This place!" he called out. "I saw him go in there."

Mawi's staff sergeant, David Kelley of Cheyenne Wells, the hammock sleeper, pulled a shotgun from his pack in the comic-book style of a sword being drawn and blasted the gate open. Mawi ran inside to find his attacker—nineteen, pubescent mustache, red and black Real Madrid tracksuit—sitting on a couch between two older women. As the women began to scream, Mawi picked up the young man and hurled him to the floor, yelling obscenities and threats[1] until Kim told him to calm down and go outside. Kelley and the others set up a guard around the house as the young man's father cried in English, "Something is wrong, something is wrong!" It was a well-to-do household. There were books and tables and sofas and

---

[1] This phrase, and much of this chapter, is taken directly from a story reported for *Time*. In that story, I did not describe how Mawi unsheathed the filleting knife he kept in a leather sheath on his chest, or how the teenager's mother anticipated blood and screamed and wept, or how Mawi brandished the knife and shouted "You try to kill me? Maybe I'll kill you. I'll kill you!" I suspect, but do not know, that the editors would have taken such information out of the piece, because it seemed too hard on the soldiers and it wasn't a big story anyway. But that was not why I omitted it. I omitted it because I talked myself into the belief that there was nothing to be gained by describing the madness and cruelty that appeared in the heat of that moment. After all, LT Kim, an intelligent officer and fundamentally decent man, had intervened, pulling Mawi off, no blood spilt. Everyone decided when to compromise. Before I arrived, a correspondent for *Time* told me that after the magazine broke the Haditha story, none of the Marines would talk to him. What you wrote was supposed to be a balancing act, access against detail. The details you left out were the ones you thought about the most.

lamps and a carpeted staircase, and Kelley said aloud, to no one really, or maybe to the uncomprehending aunts of the young attacker, "This is a nice place. What's he trying to kill us for?"

As the women stopped screaming, the soldiers zip-cuffed the young man and led him into the street. They made him kneel against a wall and swabbed his hands and pockets for residual explosive materials. The test, never famous for its accuracy, came up positive. Back in the house, a sergeant pointed this out to the young man's father. The father continued to insist that there had been some mistake.

"But we saw him, too, guy," said the sergeant.

The father would not be dissuaded. He was graying and well-dressed; now he produced his Baghdad Bar Association membership card. "I am a professor of law at the university," he said, and showed that identification also. "I am astonished this has happened. He was inside, eating. Smell his breath!"

He repeated his protests as the soldiers loaded his son into an armored personnel carrier and drove him to a nearby Iraqi National Police station. The stated mission of the U.S. military in Iraq was to support and advise the fledgling Iraqi security forces. All detainees, therefore, were supposed to be processed through the Iraqi Army or Police. Of which there were several varieties—often competing—at national and local levels.

At the station, Kim sat the young man down on the floor of IP Lieutenant Karim's office and began to question him in tandem with the Iraqis. A television played a muted Arabic melodrama in the corner. The young man denied everything. His eyes darted, periodically, to a length of rubber tubing leaning against LT Karim's desk. As the questioning continued, the Iraqis occasionally passed the tubing back and forth, and one of them whispered something into the young man's ear.

After an hour, Kim stood up to leave. He told LT Karim he would be back to check on the detainee in the morning. The detainee raised his thin arms and called out to Kim's translator, Specialist Mohammed Houbban, forty-three, of Morocco by way of Orlando. Kim and Houbban ignored him.

"He was begging to come with us," said Houbban as he walked out of the station. "And he just tried to kill us. He didn't want to be left with them." Outside, talking it over, several American soldiers agreed that the young detainee was about to be beaten.

The next day, Kim returned to the police station. LT Karim was in a good mood. He said that the detainee had been moved, but had confessed overnight. He had even offered the location of a stash of explosives, and admitted, on videotape, to shooting an Iraqi police officer in the back of the head. LT Karim hoped that he and the Americans would work together again soon. It was the first time that Kim's platoon had managed to chase down and apprehend an attacker in Ras al-Khor.

"It was a joyful moment for us," one of Kim's sergeants told me that afternoon. "We've been getting hit so much for the last few weeks." Like the rest of the men in his platoon, however, he was concerned that the detainee would bribe his way out of trouble. "You hear so many stories about how they get out," he said. "What we're worried about is, is justice gonna get served?"

He was right to worry. Bribery was everywhere. But, like many crimes, bribery was not counted as a significant act, and did not figure into the U.S. Army's metrics. And then, too, there was the simple, troubling question of who should determine "justice" in war. A father, a jury member, a general, a judge? Not long after the incident, LT Kim emailed me that the kid had been sent to Baghdad for trial. He added:

> LT Karim, from the National Police, spoke with the detainee's father today. The father was not shocked whatsoever about his son; rather, he was upset that his son admitted to committing the crimes.

XL

The clip-art posters next to the computers seemed like jokes—cartoon wagging fingers and capital letters—but really they were about controlling information. *Silence is security.* Once, trying to file a piece, I asked a sergeant running the computer shack if there was really no way I could plug my flash drive in. He seemed like he might be sympathetic, like there might be some trick to getting around the firewall or whatever it was that blocked uploads. Instead he growled, "You think *we* don't want to send pictures and shit back home?"

Almost everyone had a digital camera. They took pictures of Iraqi children in their street packs, of each other, of dead bodies, of dust storms. Maybe the sergeant was pissed he couldn't send pictures of himself to his girlfriend, the way good girlfriends sent naked pictures of themselves. Was there a possibility that someone's wife would let slip to Sunni extremists that the Cavalry was leaving Mosul? Maybe. The whole enterprise seemed haunted by the Abu Ghraib pictures. You wondered about every camera, every digital card full of potential evidence.

But in the end you didn't worry about it that much, if you were a GI, because you had to go back out in one of those humvees. It just didn't seem that important when you might get blown up. And you were just pissed off that you couldn't send pictures home, for your folks to hang on the fridge, for your dad to show his buddies, for your parole officer to laugh at.

XLI

It was all transactional, an occupation of trade-offs. One afternoon I watched a local middle-aged contractor in a corduroy suit, red-checked keffiyeh, and dark glasses climb quickly into the back of an MRAP. American soldiers favored the hulking MRAPs over lighter Humvees not only because they were more likely to survive an IED blast (the trade-off: speed for armor), but because they were more spacious—five men could sit comfortably, facing inward. It was even possible, if the jamming system was not whirring and the engine was not roaring and the mounted machine gun was not blasting, to have a meeting inside one, and this was why the contractor had come—for a meeting held in the privacy of an MRAP, where the Iraqi Army would not see money changing hands and could not try to extort the contactor, whom the U.S. had hired to remove trash from the neighborhood.

The first concern the contractor voiced, however, was not about the Iraqi Army. It was about the Americans. "We need only one thing for us," he said. "For the U.S. forces to stay away."

The contractor had brought up the issue in the first meeting, a week before. That meeting had taken place inside (rather than in the parking lot of) an Iraqi Army base, in what had once been a school. The local Iraqi Army colonel who had introduced the Americans and the contractor had quietly chaired the discussion. The contractor was concerned that he and his workers might be targeted by insurgents if they were seen to be working with the Americans. The officers in charge, Captain Burden and Lieutenant Warren of the 3rd Cavalry's

2nd Field Artillery Battalion, had promised the contractor that their patrols to check on the progress of the project would appear random and unrelated. The contractor, in turn, promised to remove every piece of trash from the neighborhood's streets and empty lots. The neighborhood, Saba Nissan, was a middle-class enclave that the U.S. military had recently "cleared" of insurgents (the captain told me they had found almost nothing in the raids). The price for the project was approximately 33,000 U.S. dollars.

In the following days, all concerned parties kept their word, sort of. The U.S. military patrols were random, but the battalion commander came by, too. And, maybe because it was the brigade's first operating civil-affairs project since it had arrived in January, so did the brigade commander. And then, because the project seemed to be going so well, so did a two-star general. In this way, the men who had made the promise unintentionally betrayed the contractor. And though while I was there no one died as a result of this betrayal, it was perhaps indicative of the way that the American Army operated. A week after the project started, the neighborhood gutters were the cleanest I had seen in Iraq outside of the Green Zone, though according to Captain Burden, the lots were only up to "Iraqi standard, not American standard."

He and Lieutenant Warren told the contractor so in the MRAP meeting, and emphasized that he would have to clean some of the lots again. The contractor agreed, but reiterated his concern about the American forces, warning that already "there were strange people driving around my employees." The captain and the lieutenant promised again that their forces would stay away. Finally, LT Warren produced a fat stack of Iraqi dinars from a black plastic bag and handed it over. The MRAP's ramp dropped, heavy and mechanized, and the contractor left, alone, headed back into the city.

I walked around the neighborhood to watch the trash getting

picked up that afternoon. "The Iraqi government is supposed to look like they're doin' it, not us," Captain Burden had told me. So I asked around to see if the captain was getting what he wanted. Some of locals knew the U.S. was behind the trash removal, while some of them did not. Likewise, some of them were extremely pleased about the clean-up, while others said they hadn't noticed. All were suspicious of me and my Army translator, Ed Abu George, fifty-one, an Arab from Kirkuk who lived in Phoenix when he wasn't working for the military. It wasn't how I wanted to report in the neighborhood—with Ed, following a squad of infantry guys—but it was a trade-off. The Army circus for security.

The last man I spoke with in the neighborhood was one Ali Salim. Ed didn't want to talk with him, but I insisted. Ali Salim was carrying some groceries home. He wore a blazer and said he owned a drugstore near Mosul University. Ed smoked and rolled his eyes while he and Salim spoke, and his translations seemed significantly shorter than Salim's answers. Soon Salim began to speak rapidly and passionately. Ed waved this talk away. I asked him to tell me exactly what Salim was saying.

"He is trying to tell me a story, of insurgents, the coalition, Iraqi Police, how they are all connected. But I told him you only wanted an answer about the trash, good or not good."

I told Ed that I wanted to hear the whole story.

Salim interrupted, in imperfect English. "How they can ask me and not want for the answer?"

"I'm sorry," Ed said to me, retrieving his pack of cigarettes from inside the U.S. Army jacket he wore. "Arabs are impossible."

XLII

Civil Affairs Lieutenant Warren spoke slowly, and wore his pistol on his chest, where it was highly visible but out of the way. The evening after that meeting in the MRAP he did hours of paperwork related to the Iraqi contractors employed to take the trash out of Rashidiya. It had been a long day. When he was finally done he stopped by the office next door, where a public-affairs officer was telling me jokes and showing me the Chuck Norris posters on the wall. Warren paused and leaned against the doorframe, sizing up the situation.

"Hey, uh," he said, pointing at stack of DVDs on the desk, "could I get a look at those?"

The public-affairs officer handed them over. Warren shuffled through the muscle-car movies and the stoner comedies and in the end chose *Bolt*, a cartoon starring a dog in a cape.

"*Bolt?*"

"I like the cartoons," said Warren.

XLIII

Everyone you met could explain why he was there.

"It is a sign of faith that we're here now," specialist Ryan Dunne told me as he stood watch over a line of detainees facing a wall in an abandoned school. "It's faith that they can do the job."

Usually the reason was simpler. *Because I'm a soldier and I follow orders.* Sometimes it was more complicated, especially for Iraqis. And they were the ones who really needed an answer, because the Americans were always asking them what they were doing here. As they walked to school, to the market, hand in hand to the mosque, on their way to weddings and funerals. The wrong answer got you facing a wall under the watchful eye of Specialist Dunne.

Most problematic for the Americans were the Iraqis who explained nothing, who simply detonated. This was of course the clearest explanation, clearer even than "I am an Iraqi, what are *you* doing here?"

And the real American answer was this: "I want to be here." Even if a few were surprised at the deployment, or were escaping some trouble back home, or were against the war. Everyone, one way or another, had signed up, even if they hadn't been thinking about what that meant. But then, the future was hard to know.

I asked Specialist Dunne about the future one day, as we watched another guy in his squad scan the eyes of a detainee across the hall. "What about after the U.S. leaves?" I said. "Do you think it'll be okay?"

He scratched one of the pimples on his cheek, under his tired, twenty-two-year-old eyes, and laughed. "They'll get invaded."

XLIV

2nd Lieutenant Max Palumbo was short, stocky, twenty-two, and spoke in a nasal South Boston accent. He did not like reporters, and his captain told me that he had embedded me with Palumbo because he thought it would be good for him to get some practice talking to the press. Told me something like, "He's gotta learn how to talk if he wants to get anywhere in the Army."

But Palumbo was already famous for the way he talked. He called everybody cocksucker, and he said it so broadly it sounded more like *caulk soccer*. The way Palumbo talked was a running joke for the other guys in his company. Loud and rude and *Bahstan*, funny every time somebody did an impression, especially if you thought about Palumbo's delicate, almost inaudibly quiet terp, Andy.

Andy was a Yazidi guy—the Yazidis being the Kurdish ethnic group that I had been told worshipped the devil. All the terps had Iraqi names, of course, like Yassem, or Uday, or Malik, but they all got renamed Ricky, or Cosmo, or Blue, or Andy. Andy really didn't look like an Andy, but he had more reasons than most for using an alias. Palumbo told me that some of the guys had come around a corner once and "caught the little *fecker* getting railed by one of the other terps." And as a Yazidi, Andy was a member of an even smaller minority than gay Iraqi terps.

"Worst terp in the *feckin'* Army, and you can't heah the little queah when he talks. *Feck*," Palumbo told me, shaking his head. The night-vision attachment to his helmet swung back and forth like a cobra head. "I hate the feckin' guy."

Palumbo seemed to hate everything. He was not even twenty-five, but he had a lot to live up to. His division antecedents had fought through Rhineland, Ardennes-Alsace, and Central Europe in World War II, and the Drang Valley in Vietnam. There in Mosul the two other lieutenants in his company had already taken contact and fired back, but Palumbo had not seen a single moment of action. He told me directly he really wanted to "take some *feckin'* contact."

Everyone I asked agreed that this was normal. The metaphor that often came up by way of explanation was that it was like training all season for the game and never getting to play. I thought about this as I watched Palumbo tell Andy to *speak the feck up* as he translated for some Iraqi police in the rubble of their car-bombed checkpoint.

"You tell them that they need anything, they call me," said Palumbo, pointing at his cell phone. "They get that?" he said to Andy. "Those *cocksuckahs* come back, they call me."

"*Cocksuckah*," said one of the Iraqi police, giving a thumbs-up, and they all laughed, even quiet Andy.

XLV

Everyone seemed to be a father. The usual demographic factors were in play. Soldiers tended to be from rural or inner-city, lower-income backgrounds. But there was so much fatherhood you got the sense that there had to be more to it than that. One explanation I got was that the twelve months between deployments was exactly the right amount of time to get a family started.

Another was that as a soldier, if you knew you were going to die, you wanted to experience fatherhood before it was all over. Another was that it was important to pass on your genes. Another was that condoms didn't feel good. Another was that if you didn't have a kid, other soldiers might think you were gay. Another, one I heard more than once, was, "Well, my dad did the same thing."

XLVI

One night on patrol Palumbo decided that a building he saw was *suspicious*. It had new locks, fresh paint, a satellite dish, and was marked with a sign he couldn't read. His Yazidi terp Andy translated it loosely as "travel agent," but Palumbo said this was *feckin' suspicious*, that the whole block was *suspicious*, because there were other travel agents around, too, signs for buses to Syria and Jordan. He talked through the suspicions as he pointed the flashlight mounted on his gun at the second-floor windows of all the buildings on the block. A lot of terrorists come in from out of the country, he said, so any place where the buses come in from Syria was suspect. *And why is all this shit so nice and new?* he wondered out loud. *Right?* He discovered a small pile of scrap metal by the back door and said *What the feck is this shit?* He was walking through the gate toward the back door and entertaining aloud the possibility of searching the house right then when a half dozen bursts of gunfire echoed down the dark avenue behind him.

"We're gonna come back and check this whole place out," he said, as he remounted and led his patrol in the direction of the shots.

A curfew was in effect. The roads were empty, and all of the windows we passed were dark. The national power grid was erratic. People called national power "Maliki power," after the increasingly authoritarian Prime Minister Nouri al-Maliki, and whenever I heard this expression I imagined Maliki, in his fierce baldness, running on a hamster wheel to keep the televisions in the offices of the Iraqi police running, as they always were, even when they were beating a detainee.

But there was no television a mile up the dark street at the Iraqi police checkpoint Palumbo found. Five men stood behind a small fire in a trashcan, a single barricade between them and the road. They were stationed at an open intersection of four alleys and a wider avenue. In the flickering light of the trash fire and the harsh beam of Palumbo's flashlight, it was clear in their faces that they had just been shot at. They said that they were shot at most nights.

That night, one of their comrades, now back at the station, had survived a round to the vest. They showed Palumbo the pockmarks in the wall behind where they stood. As Palumbo and his translator talked through what had happened, his sergeants set up security at the corners. The alleys were grim, and you could see in the way that the young men walked, looking over their shoulders at the sergeants for reassurance, that they didn't want to be in those alleys by them-selves, even with their mythological ability to see at night. The Iraqi police didn't spread out. They were all smoking together on the most protected side of the street.

Palumbo wanted to charge down the alleys after the shooters, but his platoon sergeant talked him out of that. Then he started talking about the building at the center of the intersection. It was a school, it turned out, attached to the mosque behind it. "That's the *feckin'* place," said Palumbo, "we'll get on the roof there and set up a kill zone."

His idea was to come back the next night and fake a meeting like the one he was having now. Then, when the vehicles drove off, he and a few handpicked men would get on the roof of the school at the center of the intersection and *kill some motherfuckers*. The school was locked, of course, so he'd have to break in. And if there was a night watchman, or even a family living inside, Palumbo would just have to tie them up or knock out the guard, make sure it was quiet while he waited for the bad guys. *Then we'll get the motherfuckers.*

The next day, Palumbo told me that there wouldn't be room up on the roof of the school for me, so that night I rode with the platoon sergeant. After we had deposited Palumbo and his hand-picked team at the intersection, we continued on down the street. We drove around the neighborhood a few times and then parked in the dark shadows of a highway and waited for three hours, listening to Palumbo whisper that there was no contact. They were the worst kind of whispers, scratchy and low coming through your headset, as out of some barely remembered nightmare. Palumbo clutching his gun and whispering on a roof. *Negative contact. We'll be ready. Negative contact. Negative contact.*

The platoon sergeant chuckled. He was ready to get done with this bullshit, he told me in the darkness of the truck, and get back for some midnight chow.

XLVII

Standing guard. There was one guy standing guard at COP Courage in Mosul who told me directly that he didn't want to be in Iraq. He was nineteen, from Michigan. I didn't take any notes when I spoke with him, don't even remember his name. I was supposed to be writing a story about tension between Arabs and Kurds and whether this tension would turn into civil war. This soldier didn't know anything about the politics of the country, and his disdain for all of the people who lived in it was uninformed. He wore a permanent snarl, and this was probably why his superiors had stuck him on gate duty at the COP.

"So fucking boring."

I was waiting at the gate for a ride. He sat on a folding chair with another private, smoking Newports. Their job was to open the gate when convoys arrived. There wasn't a lot to look at, once you'd been at the COP for a day, even though the main building was a former palace. Inside, a mosaic on one wall depicted Saddam with a girl on his lap—the soldiers pointed out that she looked like her hand was in his crotch. Another mosaic showed Saddam, fifteen feet tall, with one hand magnanimously on the head of an old woman in an abaya and the other hand holding a grenade. Displays of mercy and strength. The ceilings were tiled beautifully, the staircases marbled. There was a pool and a sort of mini-ziggurat pool house.

While I waited for my ride the private told me how fuckin' dirty the country was. There was trash everywhere, piled in the gutters, rolling across the road on the dusty wind. Shell casings and candy wrappers, plastic bags, cigarette butts, posters of candidates long assassinated. The dirtiness was something that everybody could agree on, even some of the Iraqis, though everyone had their own reasons for agreeing—to bond, or to get a quote, or to feed a vengeance to come.

The corollary to the "shithole trash pit" grumbling was an even more common complaint: how much the whole place stank. It wasn't like the country towns that a lot of the GIs came from, but it might not have been that different from the endless spread of highway rest stops that connected them. And really, every place smelled different. There were thousands of smells, even just on an American FOB. The funk of the rooms at what they called Motel Six. The antiseptic urine stink of the latrine units at the end of the row. The fried smell, same as anywhere else in the world, that hit you when you walked past the base Burger King. The Velcro smell of Kevlar that you only noticed when you finally took off your body armor.

As I sat listening to their complaints, I noticed a pair of armed men walking along the top of the compound wall. Looking at them was hard—they were backlit against they sky and their silhouettes burned into your eyes. I pointed them out to the guards.

Yeah, the Michigan private told me, they come walking along the wall sometimes. And at night, too. It was a strange setup, he said, because outside the East walls of the COP there was a whole other wall, higher than the first, that protected the next compound over. That compound was an even larger palace, Saddam's own summer-time palace, he'd heard, and there was an Iraqi Army Battalion head-quartered there. Those were the guys on guard duty for the Hajjis.

"And look at the fuckin' windows," he said, pointing beyond the men on the wall to the broken windows of the building behind them. "They break them in the summer to stay cool. The fuckin' idiots."

I wondered where he had gotten that. He had only deployed in December, so someone must have told him that that's why the windows were broken. We watched the pair of Iraqis turn the corner on the wall. Maybe they were talking about the windows, too. Or maybe they were talking about the enormous quantities of food that got thrown out at the COP beneath them, or the handheld video-game systems that they saw the privates playing, or about gossip from their hometowns, or about their superiors, or Iraqi politics. Or maybe they talked about how lucky they were to have guard duty on that wall between two compounds, a place where they were unlikely to get shot at or see anyone except those American kids who wouldn't even hold their gaze when they walked by every day.

XLVIII

At the end of the embed I had another interview with Colonel Gary Volesky. His public-affairs officer called it an "exit interview," and suggested that the Colonel might be interested in my opinion, as an outsider and a journalist, of what I had seen while I was with his troops. As I walked through the door Volesky rose and greeted me with the same strong handshake that he'd had the first time. In fact, he said exactly the same thing as he had the first time, except for the tense.

"You've been part of the family while you were here with the 1st Cavalry," he said, and handed me a second baseball cap.

XLIX

The next email I got with the subject heading "Basketball" wasn't from Tariq; it was from Ra'ad. I got it just before I left Mosul.

> dear nick.
>
> i do not now if u hear abot tariq. he was killed and 2 more after basketball game. please send hakim number in america. i need to help me leave soon.
>
> thank you sir.
> ra'ad

The next week, back in Baghdad, I had a whiskey one evening with the *Time* bureau manager and a pair of reporters and told them about the killings at the basketball game. I had gotten another email that day, from Hakim back in the States:

> Till the family is out and safe im hesitant to reveal any details through the media for security reasons.[2] Tariq was one of my closest friends besides being a cousin, and his family is mine. Tariq was targeted and killed as he was heading home from the basketball game while holding the ball and wearing the gear. The note accused him of promoting a US or western sport. Im sorry you did not have the chance to meet him. He is truly an extraordinary person.

---

[2] Per these security concerns, Hakim, Ra'ad, and Tariq are psuedonyms.

My colleagues had been in Iraq for a long time, and they shook their heads and agreed that there were no coincidences. It had to do with me wanting to do a story there. I was lucky not to have been there, they told me. I thought about it all for a long time, but there wasn't much more to say. It was a drop, one of thousands, millions of stories. Hakim himself had twice been kidnapped; he'd also been shot, once, by a Marine. As we smoked and switched to beer and other topics, I thought of something a journalist who had covered Rwanda once told me. He had arrived in April 1995, about a year after the genocide. He said that in an awful way it was the easiest story he had ever reported, because literally everyone he spoke to had a story. And in this way, in these places, the whole idea of stories became base and twisted. It seemed that way in my short time in Iraq. Everyone had stories, and they were all awful.

The bureau manager lit another cigarette as we sat in silence for a moment.

"And especially, basketball being a pro-Western sport was non-sense," he said. "Iraqis have been playing basketball for fifty years, since long before all this. They love it."

L

Everyone in the *Time* house agreed about the best direction to point the plastic chairs in the garden. It was actually back toward the house, so that you were looking at the pair of date palms that grew over it, and the sky beyond, rather than at the Al Hamra hotel across the street. On one of my last nights, though, I turned a chair in the garden around and looked at the hotel instead of the trees. The TV networks were based there, and on the walls the wires hung like liana in the jungle, thick and so tangled it looked impossible to undo them all. How could they ever be taken down? You would need a battalion of electricians, determined cherry pickers, to untangle each knot one by one, intrepid men certain that they would not be shot while they were suspended up in that basket, trying to maintain power so that the city could run its lights, watch its bootleg DVDs, and turn its Chinese air-conditioners on against the ancient heat. While I was there, only NBC was maintaining a permanent presence, and they were probably on the way out, too, but the wires on the wall weren't just theirs. The other networks had left wires behind. Thickets of them. The city would eat them up, eventually; they would reconstitute themselves in bits, sold across the neighborhoods when foreign journalists in Iraq were as rare and ludicrous as pterodactyls.

By then the recession had hit, and most people believed that the war was ending, or at least that the story was ending. In January of that year, the rumor went, *Time*'s Iraq budget was halved. I didn't know the precise dollar figures, but I did know that shortly before I arrived about half of the Iraqis had been let go, and that those who remained were concerned about their jobs. Like many others, the Iraqi staff for the Western media depended on the war, or perceptions of the war. *Time* would shut down the bureau in July of 2009.

That day, though, the garden was a pleasant, peaceful place to sit, even if you occasionally heard explosions. It was never really quiet. If we weren't running our own generator, other generators were running nearby. You made your peace with it if you could. I briefly knew one reporter who couldn't bear to sit in the garden with the generator running. She hated it and would retreat inside before anyone else. She was the only reporter, up till then, who ever said to me that she had "a bit of the post-trauma," and I don't know how but the two things seem connected. She was very brave and elegant and maybe she just didn't like talking over the noise, but they seemed connected.

LI

The day before I left Baghdad, I had lunch with a man in Iraqi intelligence who does not want to be named. Through a translator, we spent the afternoon talking about terrorist groups in Iraq. The terrorists, of course, don't refer to themselves as such, and the definition of that word changes depending on whom you ask. Athil al-Nujayfi, for example, was the new governor of Nineveh. His detractors pointed out that in television interviews he never used the Arabic word for terrorist—*irhabiy*. He used *mujahidin*, a more ambiguous word, open to positive interpretation, that doesn't smell as much of cordite. Several Kurdish officers in the Iraqi Army whose job it was to protect Mosul told me this was evidence that Nujayfi was beholden to terrorists—the kind of men who pay teenagers to throw grenades in the street, or blow themselves up before shrines, but prefer to be called holy warriors. The intelligence source I spent the afternoon with claimed to have intimate knowledge of such men, and described them to me as a favor to the bureau manager, with whom he had an older relationship that I did not understand and was unable to clarify with either of them.

He began with al Qaeda. A single cell, he told me, comprises a commander, a driver, and a bodyguard. For every three such cells there is a superior fourth cell composed of an administrator, an issuer of fatwas, and another commander. These twelve men, he said, are a family. Ten of these families equal a section. Each section is commanded by an emir, with his own finance, fatwa, administration, and security team. Baghdad is home to six sections, and led by a supreme emir, one Abu Omar, the "prince of Baghdad," who also controls auxiliary units with particular responsibilities: logistics, raising money through kidnapping, fighting Sunnis allied with the Americans. One month later, on the first of two days in which coordinated bombings across Baghdad would kill 150 civilians, the Iraqi military reported that they had detained Abu Omar. Extremists' websites denied his capture. The American military would neither confirm nor deny it, but then, as the *New York Times* reported, the American military believes Abu Omar to be a "fictitious Iraqi figurehead" anyway.

The source I was talking with took Abu Omar's existence for granted, and did not linger on him. Al Qaeda, he suggested, was the easy group to understand. He moved on to the Sunni groups. These are not fighting a global jihad; they are fighting for control of their country. The Iraqi Islamic Army, the Army of Mujahidin, Ansar al-Sunna, the Brigade of the 20th Revolution, the Army of Abu Bakr al Sadiq, the Islamic Front for Resistance, the Army of Rashadeen, the Army of the Brothers of Mohammed. Each is distinct. There were a few more important ones he named, but besides this core there were forty-three, he said, that in his opinion were not powerful enough to mention. He described divisions in the leadership of the major groups and their relations to members of the Iraqi parliament. He explained where each group received its funding, some from Syria, or Libya, or Saudi Arabia, or the UAE, or simply from inside Iraq. He explained that recently these groups had formed a Council for the Unification of Iraq, and were planning on secretly supporting two candidates in the coming elections. Some of the groups believe it is appropriate to kill Americans only, he said, while some believe it is appropriate to kill other Iraqis, and this was a matter of contention.

You could call a source like this by different names. A source, yes, but also a spy, an informer, a traitor, a pawn. It matters what you call him, because what you call him suggests how much you trust him—it's the difference between an *irhabiy* and a *mujahidin*. As Iraq's gains are threatened by increased violence, Americans, and people around the world, might be stopping to consider what exactly to call the situation there, if not "war." An absolute failure, maybe, or an atrocity. Some insist on calling it a victory. In light of the announced withdrawal plans—despite the possibility of a renegotiated Status-of-Forces agreement, *the real possibility that we will stay longer*—some call it old news. Most Americans just call it the Iraq War, and don't think about it that much.

The American soldiers on the ground, like the 3rd Heavy Brigade Combat Team, 1st Cavalry Division that I embedded with in Nineveh province, don't think about what to call it very much either. When they talk about the war, they tend to tell war stories, as soldiers do. On Mosul's Forward Operating Base Marez, some officers told me a new one. One of their platoons had been on patrol when they came across a few Iraqi Army soldiers who had caught a boy, he looked about fifteen, who had just set an IED. The Iraqi soldiers told him: you set it, you defuse it. So they sent the boy across the road, where he crouched and began trying to defuse the bomb he had just set. It was at this point that the American platoon leader arrived, and said to them, "What the fuck are you doing—" And then the bomb went off. The platoon's medic, miraculously, saved the boy's life, though not his right arm. And that was the end of the story. The officers had it on video, and we watched it all on a laptop. One officer laughed after it was over, shaking his head, thinking out loud. "You set the bomb," he said, "you defuse it."

So what to call Iraq, now in its seventh year of American occupation? What word to use? There wasn't really time, with the source that afternoon, to talk about it. By evening we were almost done with an outline of the Sunnis, but had not even touched on the Shia groups, an even larger part of the picture. The source quickly mentioned several of them, including the remnants of the Mahdi Army, the Iranian-trained Hezbollah paramiltaries, the Badr Brigade. But then he excused himself. He was busy, had to go, said he was leaving the country for a while himself.

I saw him the next day in the airport, and nodded, and actually sat down next to him to wait for the plane. I didn't think we'd be able to talk, of course, because he hadn't spoken any English in the interview. He leaned over.

"Would you like to join me for lunch at my house in Amman?" he said, unsmiling.

"I'm sorry," I said, "But I have plans to meet someone." Neither of us were telling the truth, exactly.

LII

For the duration of the Iraq War, we have also been fighting a war in Afghanistan. Like many journalists and soldiers, after Baghdad I relocated to Kabul for a while, to look at the new preeminent war. Eager to do the same, I discovered, was Gu, the Brazilian sergeant. Over the phone from Texas, on leave, having just rolled out of bed one afternoon, with a little under two years left on his contract, he told me this:

> I got a bunch a buddies in Afghanistan right now. Nothin' but bad news coming out of their mouths... Mom hasn't gotten her papers. We sent her back to Brazil. Fucked up on anti-depressants... I came down on orders to Alaska... Fort Wainwright. It's in the middle of nowhere... The Arctic wolves or some gay shit like that... Honestly, I want to go to Afghanistan at least once. I'm a grunt... Once you go and have actually fought you get hooked. Fucked up. I sound like a fuckin lunatic but...

I interrupted and told him that he didn't sound like a lunatic.

Some argue that every soldier is responsible for determining whether his side's role in a war is just. Others argue that the soldier's primary responsibility is to obey orders. Authority structures, social processes, Thucydides, Hobbes, Marx, Machiavelli, Gandhi. Preemptive, pacifist. And Clausewitz: "War is an act of force... which theoretically can have no limits."

Comparative inquiry into the Iraq and Afghanistan wars has been widespread, and useful to talk-show pundits and politicians and think-tank scholars. Even on call-in radio, the key distinction is the question of what is called in academia *jus ad bellum*, or justice of war. According to the latest administration, the American presence in Afghanistan constitutes a *just war* because we are not unprovoked aggressors, as we are in Iraq. Rather, we are responding directly to the attacks of September 11, 2001, which came from Afghanistan, or at least the Afghanistan/Pakistan border area.

It seems obscene to write in Latin about wars in which illiterate children gather and sell spent .50 cal casings to raise money for food. Balancing lyric and intellect, high rhetoric with grim detail, is a delicate operation, as any wartime speechwriter can tell you. But distinct from *jus ad bellum* is the notion of *jus in bello*, or justice *in* war. There is a great deal of international law and philosophy that has been written about that Latin prepositional difference. An equally important unifying idea is this: as Americans, we don't listen enough to the Iraqis, or the Afghans.

Simple but not easy. And so American combat outposts in Nawa, Afghanistan resemble combat outposts in Mosul, Iraq. Likewise similar is the relationship between U.S. servicemen and terps, whether Tajik or Kurd. Likewise do journalists in Kabul decry the increasing insularity of the U.S. diplomatic corps, just the way they did in Baghdad. Likewise the Taliban kidnap and kill civilians the way the Mahdi Army did. But apparently one war is just, and the other is not.

One of my first days in Afghanistan, I asked a fixer to show me around Kabul's bookshops, to help me learn the city. They weren't really shops, rather streetside piles, or stalls of stacked old paperbacks. We chatted with the proprietors. Along a crowded downtown avenue, one of them told me that he would rather be fighting than selling books, that he would join the Taliban and kill my people if only the Taliban weren't themselves working with the British. There was a rumor that week, fomented by President Hamid Karzai's most recent elliptical and ominous press conference, that the British had supplied the Taliban with helicopters and the insurgents were flying north to do battle outside of their traditional Pashtun bases.

The bookseller's insurgent sympathies didn't prevent him from asking me to squat on the sidewalk and drink tea. I didn't doubt, however, that he was serious about fighting Americans. He employed the strongest argument, a corollary to *do unto others*:

"What if it was your country that was invaded?"

Later, when I was off the sometimes-bombed sidewalk, unafraid of a foreign environment, back in Brooklyn, I reconsidered his question. What if the bakery down the street had been destroyed by *katyushas*? What if the traffic cops didn't speak English and were scared enough of you to pull a gun if you ran a stop sign? What if when my father had a heart attack, the hospitals were too full of gunshot casualties to treat him? What if my brother, being younger, was less likely to compromise, and became radicalized, and imprisoned? Remember the way your fist clenches and your heart speeds when you see your child fall down, or sprain his ankle playing basketball? What if the small tragedies were constantly large, and mortal? How long would your heart continue to speed, before it slowed permanently, and you, having lost so much, wanted vengeance, some kind of justice, vicious balance? What if it was you who popped up from behind a wall of sandbags, and it was your best friend, the nineteen-year-old to your left, the one you talked about your girlfriend with, who got shot in the neck, in the same place where you sang along to the radio as you drove to work?

What if it was your country that was invaded?

What if is not a strong idea. But it is still worth asking, because maybe in the asking we contribute to the possibility of sustained peace. It used to be that war was taken for granted, a state of nature beyond rule. We now insist on rules. There has been, over time, change. It seems, now, that we must wage wars, that in looking for peace we must commit acts of violence. But it is possible that this too will change, and that eventually so few will believe that violence of any kind is justified that war will cease to exist. It is more likely that you, and your children, and your grandchildren, will die violent deaths. But anything is possible. Let's see where we are. Ten months after the United States government announced its plan for the end of major combat operations in Iraq, it announced an escalation of force in Afghanistan.

A NOTE ABOUT THE EMBED

An *embed* refers to the attachment of a journalist to a military unit for a set period of time. The reporting in this essay came out of my embed with the 3rd Brigade of the United States Army's 1st Cavalry Division from 2.26.09 to 3.12.09, located in and around Mosul, a city of approximately two million people in northern Iraq.

During that time, I was attached to the three units within the Brigade. The names of the battalions bear histories of movement, deactivation, and reconstitution. They can be confusing. Within the 3rd Brigade, I was with the 1st Battalion, 12th Cavalry Regiment, or 1-12; the 3rd Battalion, 8th Cavalry Regiment, or 3-8; and the 2nd Battalion, 82nd Field Artillery Regiment, or 2-82. These battalions were each constituted of three to six companies ("Apache," "Bandit," "Cobra," and "Demon" of the 1-12, for example), and each of these companies broke down further into platoons. I typically spent my days on patrol at the platoon level.

Application for an embed goes through the Army's Public Affairs Office (PAO), first at the Multi-National Force (MNF) level, and then on down to successive commanders. My application was sponsored by *Time*. The military reserves the right to terminate an embed at any time, and in order to go, reporters must sign a contract stating, among other points:

1) All interviews with service members will be on the record unless otherwise stated by the designated PAO.

2)...Media will remain with military escorts and follow instructions regarding their activities at all times, until released.

...

5) Possession or consumption of alcoholic beverages while embedded or reporting is not authorized.

...

8) While in transit to and from an embed or unit visit, the media cannot act in a news-gathering capacity.

...

13) While covering an MNF-I unit, reporters may inadvertently be exposed to classified material... The media will adhere to the following guidelines to ensure operational security:

   ...

   b) Embargos may be imposed to protect operational security and future operations.

   ...

   d) Disagreements shall be referred to the next level of command and editors for resolution.

Profits from this book will be donated to The List Project (thelistproject.org), a nonprofit organization founded in the belief that the United States has a clear and urgent moral obligation to resettle to safety Iraqis who are imperiled due to their affiliation with the U.S. It has two pillars. One: help the hundreds of Iraqis on the organization's constantly expanding List make it to the United States through a partnership with three top law firms and more than 150 attorneys. And two: provide a "cushion" for resettled Iraqis upon their arrival to America by building an integration-support fund to help defray emergency expenses, and by helping them find meaningful employment.